Illustrator:
Wendy Chang

Editor:
Walter Kelly, M.A.

Editorial Project Manager:
Ina Massler Levin, M.A.

Editor-in-Chief:
Sharon Coan, M.S. Ed.

Art Director:
Elayne Roberts

Associate Designer:
Denise Bauer

Cover Artist:
Larry Bauer

Product Manager:
Phil Garcia

Imaging:
David Bennett
Hillary Merriman

Publishers:
Rachelle Cracchiolo, M.S. Ed.
Mary Dupuy Smith, M.S. Ed.

Middle School Advisement

Author:

Tricia Ball

Teacher Created Materials, Inc.
P.O. Box 1040
Huntington Beach, CA 92647
ISBN-1-55734-193-1

©1996 Teacher Created Materials, Inc.   Made in U.S.A.

Teacher
Created
Materials

Table of Contents

Introduction 4

Advisement Curriculum Goals 5

First Quarter 6
- Getting to Know You
- I'd Like to Introduce . . .
- The Famous Name Game
- The Name Game Relay
- Siamese Twins
- A Name by Any Other . . .
- Orientation to Our School
- School Facts
- Orientation to the Staff
- The Staff at My School
- Shaking Hands
- Be a Detective
- Be a Star
- No Difference
- In Search of . . .
- Trust and Team Building
- Blind Trust Walk
- Group Get Up
- Blind Walk Reflections
- Hunter Versus Hunted
- The Binder Reminder
- Daily/Monthly Assignment Reminders
- Life Skills Vocabulary
- Create-a Skit-Record
- Compliments
- Design a Board Game
- Acknowledging Birthdays
- Birthday Calendar
- No Homework Birthday Pass
- It Just Bugs Me
- Becoming Test Wise
- How Do You Learn?
- Self-Analysis Study
- Test-Taking Strategies
- Organizing Study Materials
- Correct Note-Taking Form
- Sample T-Diagram
- Tips for Test Taking
- Tips for Research Papers

- Research Paper Guide Sheet
- Research Report Evaluation Sheet
- Getting Ready for Second Quarter
- First Quarter Student Survey
- Write Your Epitaph
- Sample Epitaphs
- My Own Epitaph

Second Quarter 84
- My Problem Is . . .
- I've Got a Problem
- Treasure Hunt
- All About Me!
- Understanding Myself
- Would You?
- What I Am Not . . .
- Can I Do Better Next Time?
- Reflection Activity Sheet
- I Have a Right to Feel Good . . .
- I Am Unique
- Using Your Senses
- How Well Do You Listen?
- How to be a Good Listener
- I Hear You!
- How Do You Learn?
- Brain Facts
- The Brain
- Right Brain/Left Brain
- Self-Assessment for Right/Left Brain . . .
- Seven Styles of Learning
- Seven Intelligences Questionnaire
- Seven Types of Intelligence
- Goal-Setting Activity

Third Quarter 114
- I Am What I Am
- Mistakes in Relating
- May I Join Your Group?
- If You Can't Say Anything Nice . . .
- Self-Portrait
- If Johnny Jumps . . .
- A Coat of Arms
- My Coat of Arms
- Peer Pressure

Table of Contents *(cont.)*

- Relationships
- Evaluating Your Relationships
- Friendship
- What Makes a Friend?
- Friendship Activity
- A Picture Is Worth a Thousand Words
- A Collage of Famous Friends
- Decisions, Decisions
- Banishing Bad Habits
- Good Decisions for Bad Habits
- Make the Right Choice
- Up in Smoke or Down the Drain
- Research and Write
- Human Body Research Paper
- Research Paper Format
- The Title Page
- Note Cards
- Model Entry
- The Outline
- The Body of the Research Paper
- The Footnotes
- Acting It Out
- What Would You Do?
- Rules for Debating
- Debate Summary Sheet
- Gangs
- Families and Gangs
- Conflict Resolution
- I Admire. . .
- Goal Setting

Fourth Quarter 179
- Working Out Problems
- That's a Load off My Mind
- It's a Problem for Me
- Real Life Problems
- I Am Innocent
- Are You Doing the Right Thing?
- Looking Toward the Future
- Walking Down Life's Path
- Fame and Fortune
- My Career Choice
- After I Am Gone

- My Family Tree
- My Past, Present, and Future
- Career Orientation and Planning
- Want Ads
- Create an Ad
- Career Choices
- What Do Your Parents Do?
- Invitation to a Guest Speaker
- Job Hunting—The Interview
- Interview Questions
- Writing a Résumé
- Résumé Outline
- Sample Résumé
- Why School?
- My School's Report Card
- Aw, Mom, Do I Hafta Go to School?
- The Ideal School
- School and Career Choice

Multicultural Projects for the Year 233
- The Ramadan Fast and Id-Ui-Fitr
- Map of Moslem Countries
- Flags of Moslem Countries
- Tet-Trung-Thu
- Mexican Independence Day
- Mexican Independence "Torito"
- American Indian Day
- Rosh Hashanah and Yom Kippur
- Oktoberfest
- El Dia de los Muertos
- Diwali
- Loy Krathong
- Mardi Gras
- Mardi Gras Mask
- Arbor Day
- Urini Nal

Glossary 253

Bibliography 265

Appendix 267
- Teacher Savers
- Awards

Introduction

You have been asked to teach an advisement program to your middle school students, and you need some advice yourself as to what to teach and what to advise. If that is the case, this book is for you. *Middle School Advisement* will provide a year-long program loaded with hands-on activities geared to middle school students.

This book is divided into the traditional four-quarter school year but can easily be adapted to any school year configuration. The individual activities are designed so that the teacher may choose to use them in order or individually. Some of the activities are year-long, providing the students with those skills needed to become independent workers and thinkers.

Integrated throughout this book are activities that will stimulate the students' independence, reinforce positive behaviors, and provide an opportunity for self-awareness. Generally speaking, the activities will fall into one of three categories: life skills, study skills, and goal-setting skills.

Life Skills

Life skills activities cover a wide range of topics touching on many of the day-to-day situations the students will encounter. It is important as a teacher not to overlook the fact that today many of the students we teach are left on their own while parents are at work. These children face many situations that need special skills to handle. These range from making the right decisions on a daily basis to saying no to drugs and peer pressure. From the first day of school to adulthood, the activities provided will assist in making the student a more productive part of society. Some of the many areas these activities cover are skills in problem solving, conflict resolution, communications, friendships, responsibilities, and cultural awareness.

Study Skills

Study skills provide the students with many of the tools they need to do their best in school. Many students in middle school are overwhelmed by having multiple teachers as well as an increased work load. Skills in time management, goal setting, test taking, and learning provide the students with the necessary tools to make middle school less stressful. Students will also learn how they acquire knowledge so that they can determine how they learn best.

Goal-Setting Skills

Each quarter the students are taught a different goal-setting technique. Throughout the first two quarters the students are given activities in time management, school rules and policies, and behavior modification techniques. During the second semester an emphasis is placed on cultural awareness, stereotyping, peer pressure, gangs, and drugs. Students are provided with opportunities to research and reflect upon which skills aid them in making the right decisions in their lives. Lastly, the school year finishes with activities for career awareness and planning for the future. Here is an opportunity for your students to meet business, professional, and political leaders in their community. Talking with role models gives the students a sense of some possible career choices they might pursue in later years.

Advisement Curriculum Goals

The following are goals that middle school classes should strive to meet.

- Build a trusting relationship among peers, parents, and teachers.

- Create a positive and caring school/classroom environment.

- Assist students to understand and accept limits and rules that are consistently reinforced.

- Build an awareness of unique, personal qualities.

- Promote attitudes of cooperation and acceptance of all cultures.

- Provide opportunities to discover interests, capabilities, and backgrounds of others.

- Develop self-awareness and friendship-making skills.

- Enhance ability to make decisions and seek positive alternatives.

- Teach the steps to successful goal setting.

- Aid in charting present and past academic and behavioral performances.

- Provide opportunities to increase awareness of individual competencies and strengths.

- Teach how to record and evaluate progress.

- Provide feedback on how to recognize weaknesses and profit from mistakes.

- Teach alternatives for conflict resolution among peers.

- Teach the importance of self-praise for accomplishment.

FIRST QUARTER

Ice Breakers

- Getting to Know You
- Building Relationships
- Building Trust and Teams

Life Skills
Study Skills
Goal Setting

Getting to Know You

When new students enter school with trepidation and anxiety, getting kids together—especially middle school kids—is no easy task. Many old friendships will be renewed after the long summer break, but there will be students new to the area or just entering a new school (as in the case of sixth graders) who may not feel comfortable in their new surroundings. The following activities are designed to make all students feel at home and get to know each other. They are non-stressful and fun. Some activities require a full period; others can be used at the beginning of a session as ice breakers to put your students at ease. Most of these activities provide easy ways for students to learn about their classmates and establish a basis for common interests which might promote lasting friendships. In all cases these activities are a relaxing way to get acquainted for both the teacher and students. The activities are arranged for a new group of students entering school but can be adapted in whole, in part, or in any order, as the teacher judges best.

I'd Like to Introduce . . . is excellent for opening day. What begins as a standard stand-up-and-say-your-name activity becomes the highlight of the day with many students wanting to introduce everyone in the class from memory! One student introduces himself/herself and states a memorable personal fact or characteristic. The next student must introduce the student prior and all who came before, pointing to each student in turn; then the speaker must add his/her name and memorable fact to the list. Most middle school students love this type of memory game and really become involved in learning classmates' names.

The Famous Name Game is another student favorite. It is a take-off on a popular party game and provides students a chance to use their knowledge of famous people and their skills of investigation. The teacher has the option of restricting the topics to famous people in history, authors, scientists, or other groups of persons.

The Name Game Relay is a way to relieve first day jitters and to build cooperative groups. This physical education activity is a relay race with a twist. Students are asked to provide a word in the writing of a sentence. When each student has written a word, the team should have a grammatically correct sentence on their sheet.

Orientation to Our School helps students to become aware of the physical layout of their new school and to map their way from class to class. This activity should be followed by **Orientation to the Staff** so that students may also become acquainted with school personnel.

Be a Star offers the students an opportunity to reflect on the events in their lives. A bulletin board display is an excellent way for the students to know each other.

The remaining activities are just as exciting and fun for the student and the teacher. So share your warmth, your spark, and your enthusiasm with your new students and have a successful year.

I'd Like to Introduce . . .

The teacher starts this activity by stating his/her name and telling one memorable thing about himself/herself. The teacher then chooses one student to repeat the procedure. It sounds easy, but the student must first repeat the teacher's name and what was unique about that person. The introductions continue until everyone has spoken, repeating information about each prior person.

Obviously, this is quite a test of memory, and it is the teacher's option to allow names and facts to be written down or require them to be committed to memory. The following "I'd Like to Introduce . . ." fact sheet is provided to record names and facts. After the students complete this activity, the fact sheets can be expanded by allowing time for the students to get additional information about each other and to converse about common interests. Telephone numbers can provide students with a person to call if they are absent.

Name of Teacher _____

Memorable Fact _____

Name of Classmate _____

Memorable Fact _____

Address_____

Telephone Number _____

Name of Classmate _____

Memorable Fact _____

Address_____

Telephone Number _____

Name of Classmate _____

Memorable Fact _____

Address_____

Telephone Number _____

Name of Classmate _____

Memorable Fact _____

Address_____

Telephone Number _____

Name of Classmate _____

Memorable Fact _____

Address_____

Telephone Number _____

The Famous Name Game

During this activity your students will try to guess the famous person's name that has been attached to their backs. Using the coupons below, write in the name of a famous person. This person can be from a certain period of time, a person alive or dead, or any person the student or teacher desires. There are no rules for the names chosen except that they be reasonably recognizable by all participants. The students then may ask questions of each other to see if they can deduce who the famous person might be. Questions may only be answered with a "YES" or a "NO."

Teacher's Note: You may choose to add the following clues to the student's cards.

I live(d) in the present (or past).

I live(d) in _____ area of the country (world).

My occupation is _____ .

This game may be adapted to any subject or theme desired.

I am	**I am**	**I am**	**I am**
I am	**I am**	**I am**	**I am**
I am	**I am**	**I am**	**I am**
I am	**I am**	**I am**	**I am**

The Name Game Relay

This is an outdoor relay game involving team cooperation and lots of room to run.

Materials Needed

- large size butcher paper—18" x 24" (45 cm x 60 cm) or larger (one per team)
- markers—one per team
- masking tape

How to Play

1. Divide your class into four or five groups. Larger classes can be divided into more teams as long as they are of equal size.

2. Put large 18" x 24" (45 cm x 60 cm) sheets of butcher paper (one per team) on the wall of the building (outdoors) or on the wall of a fairly large-sized room in your school. The gym or cafeteria work well if the weather is inclement.

3. Distribute the markers to each leader and line the teams up behind each leader about 20 feet (6 meters) from the wall.

4. Have each team member run to the wall and write a word on the team's paper. Each successive team member is to run to the wall and add a word to the sheet. When each member of the team returns to the line, the next person may go.

Object of the Game

The object of the game is to be the first team to complete the run and to successfully write a complete, logical sentence on the paper.

This game is sure to become a favorite of your students.

Siamese Twins

This is another get-acquainted game that becomes a year-long favorite. It involves two students pretending that they are Siamese twins. They stand before the class with arms locked, and the students ask them questions about themselves.

Sounds simple! However, each half of the joined twins may say only one word at a time. When the students become tongue tied or laugh too hard, they are asked to sit down and another set of twins takes their place.

Siamese twins can be used to learn newly taught materials or to review material for a test. Siamese twins is also a great activity when you have those extra few minutes to fill.

A Name by Any Other . . .

This is an art and writing activity that encompasses your students' names, their creativity, and their conception of themselves.

Materials for Each Student

- white construction paper cut into 8" x 10" (20 cm x 25 cm) sheets
- assorted colored markers, crayons, or colored pencils
- string or yarn
- hole punch

Optional: assorted lettering stencils in different type styles (Students enjoy tracing their names in various styles of writing. This also reflects the students' image of themselves.)

Procedure

Holding the paper lengthwise, have the students write their names vertically on the paper.

Instruct the students to write a phrase or a sentence about themselves, using the letters of their names.

Have them color the letters of their names in different designs.

Hang the designs over each student's desk for a colorful room display. This also helps you to learn the names of the students in your class.

Sample:

Mathematics wizard

Amiable

Responsible

Yearns to be a teacher

Orientation to Our School

Time Needed: varies with the size of the school

Materials

- an outline map of your school

Procedure

Distribute a map of the school to each of your students. Have them provide their own pens or pencils.

Take a tour of your campus. Make stops at all the important places that your students need to know. The rest rooms, water fountains, and the cafeteria are always the most important to the students, but do not overlook the location of classrooms, music rooms, the gym, the office, and other areas you feel your students might need to know.

As the group reaches each area, have the students record the name or names of those staff members who work there and what their responsibilities are. When the tour has been completed, provide any additional information the students need to know about the school and have them place it on the maps.

Punch holes in the maps and have the students place them in their notebooks.

Draw or paste a picture of your school below. On the following page, complete the "School Facts" information.

School Facts

Complete the following facts about your school.

Name of my school_____

Address _____

Telephone number _____

Homework hot line telephone number_____

The age of your school building_____

How did your school get its name? _____

What building materials went into the construction of your school? _____

_____

How far is your school from your home? _____

On the back of this paper, draw a map showing the route you take to and from school.

What are your school buildings' good qualities? _____

_____

What improvements would you like to see at your school? _____

_____

Do the conditions found at your school promote learning?_____

If you had the power to make physical improvements to your school and the school grounds, what would they be and why?_____

_____

Draw the improvements below.

Orientation to the Staff

Time Needed: 30 minutes

Activity

This activity can be managed in two ways, depending upon the size of your school.

Small School: Have various school staff come into your room and talk about their roles at school. Have personnel discuss what their duties are and what area of the school they work in. Some students never get to meet office staff, cafeteria personnel, or custodial staff. Having this personal contact also allows the student to gain additional respect for the staff and what they do.

Large School: Since large schools have numerous employees, having each person visit your class would take an unrealistic amount of time. This activity can be effectively done using old yearbooks. First, distribute the yearbooks. Then announce the name of a staff member. Students are then to find the picture in the yearbook, thus locating a face to associate with the name. The teacher can provide a brief description of the staff member's responsibilities and where that person can be found during the school day. Even returning students love this activity. It gives them a chance to see pictures of older siblings or friends and also the changes in dress, hair, and styles from year to year.

Whether you are in a large or a small school, it is important to include yourself in this activity. Students enjoy hearing about their teachers' personal lives, what activities they like, and what their home life is like. (There is no reason to become too involved about your private life, of course; just a general picture of who you are will suffice.)

Follow-Up

1. Have the students write the names of those people they will meet this year. Have them identify a distinguishing characteristic of that person so that they can remember the face (eyeglasses, curly hair, color of hair, etc.). Keep the list in a handy and safe spot in their binders.

2. Have the students write the names of staff members in their classrooms or the area in which they work on their school maps.

3. Review procedures for fire drills and duck-and-covers. Review any other drills your school might have.

4. Review the school rules of conduct and dress.

5. Instruct the students on any procedures they need to follow. Some schools have a standardized style for the students to head their papers for all written work.

The Staff at My School

Position	Duties	Location on Campus	Notes
Principal			
Vice-Principal			
Attendance Personnel			
Activities Director			
School Nurse			
Librarian			
Custodian			
Lunch Personnel			
Athletics Director/Coaches			

Add any additional people who are important at your school below.

Shaking Hands

Since most teachers in the middle school have anywhere from 60–150 students, it is difficult to know and interact with each student personally. We become busy completing the lessons we have prepared. If you feel you are too busy to take the time needed to shake hands with your students, remember this:

Handshaking helps me to become a better teacher because I am reminded that I do not teach lessons; I teach lessons to people! Shaking hands effectively is a powerful communication tool!

What the teacher says and does:

1. Explain to your students how difficult it is with so many pupils to know each one of them as well as you would like. In an effort to do this you would like to shake their hands on a daily basis.

2. Let students know that you would really like to have physical and eye contact with them every day. Explain that when they enter the room you want them to shake your hand and say "Hello." (An alternative is to gently touch them on the shoulder and say "Hi.") Some students may feel uncomfortable with touching at first. If they do not come to you, be sure to go to them some time during the period. A smile and an approving nod can be very rewarding to the student.

3. Demonstrate effective handshaking techniques for your students. Teach them to make sure the insides of their thumbs go all the way to the insides of the other people's thumbs. Explain that in order to avoid passing germs, we should not shake hands if we are feeling ill. On those days a simple nod would be acceptable.

4. If you desire, a cheery "Good Morning" may be substituted for the handshake, but personal contact is still the best means of befriending your students and making them feel welcome throughout the year.

What the students do:

1. To be honest, most students will look oddly at you the first few days. Some students will resist, but for the most part they will seek you out due to the novelty of the situation.

2. Be patient! Even the most standoffish student will melt and go along with their peers. Most middle school students do not like to be different.

3. Some students will invent their own handshakes. It may be strange at first for you, but take the time to learn them. These students are just asserting their individuality.

4. Some students may try to become too friendly. In that case maintain your professional demeanor and explain that a handshake a will do.

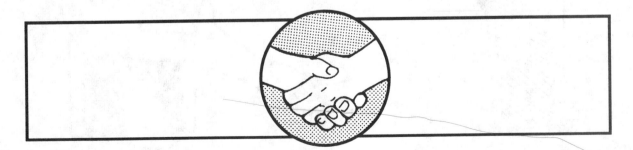

Shaking Hands *(cont.)*

Helpful Hints

1. Always keep within the comfort zone of your students and yourself. Allow the students to make handshaking a choice rather than a requirement.

2. If you are a teacher and have not yet learned how to give real handshakes, learn now! Both sexes dislike the "wimpy" handshake. This does not mean you have to squeeze your students' hands until the bones crunch, but you should offer a firm grasp.

3. Some students have sweaty palms. It happens, but try not to react to this. It will only cause embarrassment to the student and undermine your good intentions. Practice your acting skills to avoid making faces.

4. Be waiting at the door as your students come in. That way you can "physically" meet your class each day.

5. Get your students in the habit of walking in with a free right hand. That means carrying backpacks on the backs and books in the left hand.

6. Remember it takes about 30–60 seconds to greet each student each day. Those moments can be the most successful of your teaching day.

Be a Detective

Time Needed

30–50 Minutes depending on the size of the class.

Materials

- Be a Detective activity sheet for each student.

- pen or a pencil

Goal

to help students get acquainted and learn something new about their classmates

Procedure

1. Say to the students that today they are going to be detectives.

2. They are to walk around the room and question others until they find someone who has done what the question asks.

3. When they find that person, they are to write his/her name on the line.

4. They are finished when their sheet is filled or no one in the room meets the criteria for the question asked.

Closure

1. Review the question sheet with the class. It is always fun to hear the answers and to learn the names and some background about the students. This sharing also allows the students to find others with similar interests.

2. Have a reward on hand for the student who completes the entire activity sheet or the one who completes the most blanks.

Be a Detective *(cont.)*

Find classmates who fit the descriptions below. Have them sign on the appropriate line. Find someone who . . .

plays the violin_____

owns the most unusual pet _____

rides a horse _____

has visited New York _____

snow skis_____

is a Trekkie _____

speaks a foreign language _____

has lived in at least three different states _____

has the largest number of brothers and sisters _____

has an unusual hobby_____

owns the most pets_____

has been to the opera_____

has three or more pets _____

is the oldest in the class _____

is a twin _____

collects stamps _____

has always lived in the same house _____

was born in a foreign country _____

has the longest last name_____

lives the farthest from school _____

has never been in a plane_____

has a sea shell collection _____

likes spinach _____

Be a Star

Objective
Students will identify important but positive events or experiences in their lives.

Adolescents can learn to accept themselves and also learn to respect their peers by identifying important events in their lives. Adolescents need to reflect on their past. This process aids the students to realize their possibilities.

Materials for Each Student
- Use the "Stars" provided on the following page or white construction paper cut into 4" x 4" (10 cm x 10 cm) squares. Each student will be using four to five squares, so be sure to cut enough for all and some extra for those who make mistakes or might need one extra square. Try not to limit the students' creativity.
- assorted sheets of colorful wrapping paper
- glue
- scissors
- assorted markers, crayons, and colored pencils

Procedure
1. Explain to the students that they are to create a picture strip about themselves.
2. Tell the students that their strip may contain the following elements:
   - things about themselves
   - an important event of their lives
   - birth date
   - special achievements
   - trips
   - a memorable moment
   - something interesting about their lives
   - an overview of their lives
   - siblings or other family members
   - hobbies
   - an important educational experience
3. Instruct the students to draw on each star or square one picture of each event they have chosen.
4. When the five stars or squares are completed, tape or glue them into one continuous strip.
5. Using the wrapping paper, cut a star large enough to encompass the entire strip and mount the strip on the star with glue.
6. Display the strip in your class or at Back-to-School Night.

A variation of this project is to create the strips at the end of the school year to depict highlights of your students' year.

Extension
This activity is adaptable to many situations. Some suggestions are the following:
- An interview with a grandparent
- An event in history
- A literary characterization
- A current event newspaper report

Be a Star

Cut each star carefully on the lines. Then attach them to each other by lining up the points.

No Difference

Objective

The students will increase in the understanding of themselves and their peers. This activity will help in the development of interpersonal relationships and promote positive self-esteem.

Materials

- copy of the poem "No Difference" by Shel Silverstein, *Where The Sidewalk Ends,* Harper & Row Publishers, Inc., New York, 1974, page 81, and the activity sheets (pages 24–26) for each student.

Activity

1. Distribute copies of the activity sheet to your students.

2. Instruct them to listen carefully to your reading of the poem. Instruct them to think about what the poem says and then answer the questions on the activity sheet.

3. Tell students that there will be a discussion of their responses after everyone has completed the activity. (Some students might respond differently if they believe you are the only one seeing their answers.)

4. Begin the class discussion by relating something personal about yourself. For example you might relate that you are more than just a teacher. You are a wife/husband, father/mother, sister/brother, child, etc. If you speak about yourself, revealing your many roles, students may be less reluctant to speak about themselves. Ask them to reflect about their feelings towards others and how their feelings might affect others.

Closure

Ask the students to use poetry books or anthologies to find more poems or sayings about self-concept and personal identity. Have students copy them for display in the classroom.

Discuss the meanings of the poems and sayings that they found.

No Difference *(cont.)*

Listen carefully to your teacher read the poem "No Difference" by Shel Silverstein

Respond to the following questions:

1. What is the message of the poem?

   _____

   _____

   _____

   _____

2. What were your thoughts while the poem was being read?

   _____

   _____

   _____

   _____

3. What do you think Mr. Silverstein was trying to say?

   _____

   _____

   _____

   _____

4. Who do you think you are?

   _____

   _____

   _____

   _____

5. How do you think of people?

   _____

   _____

   _____

   _____

6. Is it important what other people think of you? Why or why not?

   _____

   _____

   _____

   _____

No Difference *(cont.)*

Respond to the following questions:

7. What has been or is the best part of your life?

_____

_____

_____

_____

8. What is the importance of knowing who you are?

_____

_____

_____

_____

9. How do you think other people see you?

_____

_____

_____

_____

10. Is this the image you want people to have of you?

_____

_____

_____

_____

11. Do you feel that society needs to change its attitudes about people?

_____

_____

_____

_____

12. How do you think society can accomplish this feat?

_____

_____

_____

_____

No Difference *(cont.)*

Respond to the following questions:

13. If you had the power to wave a magic wand over our world, what would the world be like? Describe your world in the space provided below.

_____

_____

_____

_____

_____

_____

_____

_____

_____

Draw a picture of something positive in your world.

Remember:

You are a valuable and important person to your friends, your family, and your world.

In Search of . . .

Objective

The students will learn the meanings and origins of their given names and surnames and other personal information related to their birth dates.

Materials

- books or sources to permit students to research the meanings of their names (Name-your-baby books are excellent sources for this activity.)

- construction paper

- markers or colored crayons or pencils

- string to hang name banners if desired.

- copies of the In Search of . . . Activity Sheets for each student.

Activity

1. Explain to students that their names are important possessions. This activity will enable them to become *etymologists*. An etymologist is a person who studies the origins and meanings of words.

2. Explain to the students that our names provide a personal or special identity. Each student has a given or a special name that identifies that person as an individual and a surname to identify the person as part of a family. All names have special meanings. Many kings, queens, and persons of power were given names that reflect their birthright.

3. Tell the students that their birth dates may also take on special meaning and that they might want to research those dates too.

Closure

Have each student research the important events that took place on the day in which he or she was born. Researching old newspapers in the library might prove quite intriguing to them.

Students might also wish to look at what took place on their birth dates for the following categories:

   a. Sporting events

   b. National or international events

   c. People in the news

   d. Weather conditions

   e. Social events

   f. Good buys or special sales on things they might purchase today (A comparison math lesson may be developed for this.)

   g. Horoscope for the day

   h. A history portfolio containing pertinent information about the day of the student's birth can be constructed. Drawings of the styles of hair and fashion can be included.

In Search of . . . Activity Sheet

1. Write your given name and surname.

   _____

   _____

   a. For whom were you named? Explain.

      _____

      _____

   b. Does your name fit you? Why or why not?

      _____

      _____

   c. Do you like your name? Explain.

      _____

      _____

   d. How did your parent(s) decide upon your name?

      _____

      _____

   e. If you could have named yourself, what would your name be? Why?

      _____

      _____

2. What does each of your names mean?

   _____

3. Make a list of some famous people who share your name.

   _____   _____

   _____   _____

   _____   _____

4. Find names that are *palindromes* and make a list of them.

   _____

   _____

   (Examples: Eve, Otto)
   Palindromes are names or words that are spelled the same frontwards and backwards. There are also palindromes that are phrases or sayings. An example is "Madam, I'm Adam."

5. After researching the information about your name, how do you feel about your name?

   _____

   _____

In Search of . . . a Logo

Many businesses today have logos that are commonly associated with their names. Examples: Walt Disney Company, McDonald Corporation, and the television stations with stylized call letters, etc.

When a person has a logo, we call it a *monogram*. A monogram is the stylistic portrayal of a person's initials. Read about monograms in an encyclopedia and create your own monogram below.

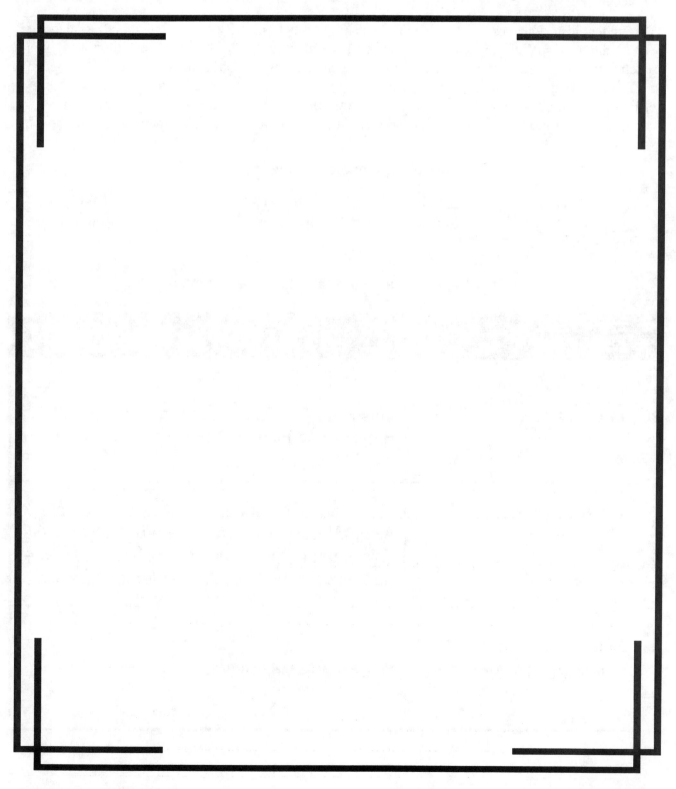

In Search of . . . the History of My Name

In early times individuals were often known by a first name only—for example, *John*. Thus John's child (named Bill) would become known as Bill, John's son. Eventually, he became Bill Johnson. This evolution explains the surnames of millions of people today—even for women, who are obviously not "sons." For an interesting parallel in the use of the word *daughter,* you might research women's names in Iceland.

Throughout history names have evolved from a simple way to identify certain individuals to elaborate combinations of spelling and sounds that make a person unique in society. Years ago it was common practice to name a child after a mother, father, or a close relative. Today many children are named after a place or a song or a feeling. You might know people with names like Sunshine, Mercedes, Chastity, or Faith. You might even have a creative name yourself. So begin your search of your name by completing the following activity sheet and speaking to your parents and grandparents to learn how your name came to be.

Sample Completed Activity Sheet

Name:	**Brian**	**Alexander**	**Johnson**
	Given	Given (middle)	Surname

History, Meanings, and Interesting Information

Names	History/Meaning/Information
Given: Brian	This is an Old Testament name, common for Bretons and Irish.
Given: Alexander (middle)	This means "defender of man, helper of man." Also, "Alysaundere" means herb in Macedonia. This is the name for horse parsley. The name was made popular by Alexander the Great.
Surname: Johnson	This means "son of John."

30

In Search of . . . My Name Makes Me Unique

Complete the following activity sheet.

Name: _____ _____ _____
                 Given   Given (middle)   Surname

History, Meanings, and Interesting Information

Names	History/Meaning/Information
Given:	
Given: (middle)	
Surname:	

In Search of . . . More Name Knowledge

Phone Search

Look in your local phone directory for names that originated because of reference to the offspring of a person or as reference to the person's trade. You will be surprised at how many there really are. List as many different ones as you can below.

Offspring	Trade or Profession

In Search of . . . More Name Knowledge *(cont.)*

School Survey

Make a list of the names in your classes. Circle the names that are most frequently used. Next, construct a bar graph of the five most frequently occurring names in your list.

Names

_____ _____ _____

_____ _____ _____

_____ _____ _____

_____ _____ _____

_____ _____ _____

_____ _____ _____

_____ _____ _____

_____ _____ _____

_____ _____ _____

_____ _____ _____

Frequency Graph

In Search of . . . More Name Knowledge *(cont.)*

Changing Popularity

Look in a name-your-baby book for some histories of names. You may be surprised to learn that some names flourish in certain generations but are almost unheard of in others. List some of those names below and report to your class, explaining the names and the times when they were popular and not popular. Try speculating as to the reasons for the continuing popularity of some names along with the reasons for some names dropping out of common use.

Popular Now	**Possible Reasons for Changing Popularity**
_____	
_____	
_____	
_____	
_____	
_____	
_____	
_____	
Popular Then	
_____	
_____	
_____	
_____	
_____	
_____	
_____	
_____	

Trust and Team Building

Objectives

- to value being accepted by a group
- to appreciate team participation
- to demonstrate commitment
- to increase trust within a group
- to improve group cooperation
- to improve problem-solving skills
- to improve communication skills
- to enhance self-esteem
- to practice the social skill of encouragement
- to become less inhibited in front of a small or a large group

Each of the following initiatives and activities is designed to meet the above objectives. The teacher's role is to act as leader and to pose challenges to the group: let the group problem-solve through oral communication and trial and error; step in only if there is a snag in the group's ability to perform the task at hand. At the end of each activity, the teacher should lead a debriefing session.

Debriefing:

Debriefing should be connected to the whole adventure experience. The debriefing period allows the group to come forth with their perceptions and thinking as much as possible, explore their feelings, and build up their own collections of observations.

There should be a basic question-sequence to debriefing: What?, So what?, and Now what?

What? refers to the substance of the group interaction and what happens to the individuals.

So What? obviously leads to a discussion of the significance or importance of the activity and objective.

Now What? should lead to a discussion of follow-up implications, further questions, and suggestions for all involved.

Examples:

- Go Around—Everyone gives one word or one descriptive sentence.
- The Memory Game—Explain in detail everything that happened. Others may interject to add details. Talk in the present tense . . . "I am," etc.

Blind Trust Walk

Objective

to develop trust in your fellow classmates

Activity

This activity can be used with groups of two or three people. Usually this activity is conducted with music being played. When you decide to change leaders, you simply stop the music being played, make the desired changes, and then continue the music.

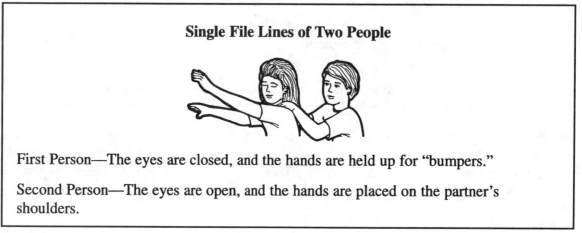

Single File Lines of Two People

First Person—The eyes are closed, and the hands are held up for "bumpers."

Second Person—The eyes are open, and the hands are placed on the partner's shoulders.

Action

Lead your blind partner in several directions with verbal and hand gestures. Next, try leading your partner without any verbal cues.

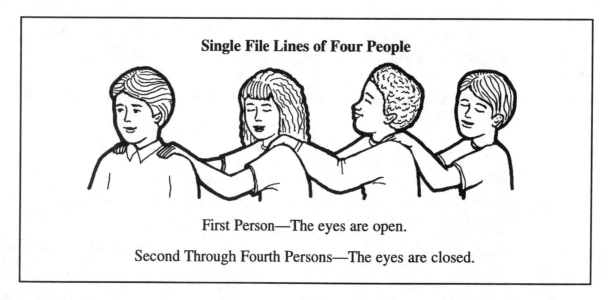

Single File Lines of Four People

First Person—The eyes are open.

Second Through Fourth Persons—The eyes are closed.

Action

All except the leader place their hands on the shoulders of the person in front. The leader leads the line without giving any verbal cues. The line is led by using body language and pressure of touch on the shoulders. When the music stops, change leaders.

36

Group Get Up

Objective

to promote group cooperation

(This activity provides the opportunity for students to realize that great things can be accomplished if they all cooperate and work as a team.)

Materials

- large clothesline rope that has been tied together at the ends and placed on the ground in a circle.

Activity

All students sit in a circle with their feet stretched out in front of them, holding on to the rope. On command, everyone pulls back on the rope and tries to stand up at the same time. Several attempts may be necessary for successful completion of this task.

Variation: Blind Walk

Objective

This simple activity will strengthen the bonds formed among your students and serve as a lesson on tolerance as well.

Materials

- four-foot lengths of clothesline for each pair of students
- handkerchief, scarf, or a suitable blindfold

Activity

Blindfold one student's eyes in each pair. Have the seeing student lead the blind student through the classroom. Ask the other students not to make a sound during this activity so that the unsighted students may use their other senses and become accustomed to relying on a partner. After five minutes have the students switch places and repeat the activity.

Blind Walk Reflections

Complete the Blind Walk Reflections survey below. Be prepared to discuss your answers with the class.

- Describe how you felt when you were blindfolded.

  _____

  _____

- Did you trust the person leading you? Why or why not?

  _____

  _____

- What senses did you use to make your way through the room?

  _____

- After the first few minutes, did you begin to trust your leader? Why or why not?

  _____

  _____

- Did you find yourself feeling about with your hands and arms, even though the leaders were told not to let you bump into anything?

  _____

- Could you sense where you were in the room?

  _____

- Do you think things might have felt different if there had been noise and people talking in the room?

  _____

- How did you feel about relying upon another person for your well-being?

  _____

- If you were the first to have your eyes covered, did your attitude change when it became time for you to become the leader?

  _____

  _____

- If you were the leader first, how might you have done things differently if you had been blindfolded first?

  _____

  _____

- Do you feel differently about handicapped people now that you were handicapped yourself?

  _____

Hunter Versus Hunted

Objective

to provide students an opportunity to rely on their senses and their wits to survive the game

Materials

- a caveman-style club constructed from butcher paper and taped closed

Activity

1. Divide the class into two equal groups. Have the groups sit opposite each other on the floor of the gym or a multipurpose area. This game is best when played indoors.

2. The teams should be approximately 20–30 feet apart.

3. Explain to the class that you are going to choose two students who will leave the line as quietly as possible to seek the club somewhere on the floor. The first one to find the club becomes the hunter. The other student becomes the hunted.

4. Sounds easy? The hitch of the game is that all participants must start the game with eyes closed; the hunter and the hunted must have their eyes closed or blindfolded at all times.

5. Explain that when one of the students locates the club, you will announce it. It is then up to the hunter to stand and walk around to find the prey.

6. The object of the game is for the hunted to find the hunter's space in line before the hunter finds him.

7. Once the hunter and the hunted have been chosen, the other students may open their eyes and observe "the hunt." The teacher announces "The club has been found. Let the hunt begin."

8. Sideline students may NOT make any noise or movements except to hold their arms out if the hunted is going to crawl or walk into them.

9. Allow a full session of time for this game. The students enjoy it, and all want their turns at being the hunter/hunted.

10. Remember to debrief. Ask what kinds of strategy were used to play and win the game.

This activity makes a great rainy day game for all age groups.

The Binder Reminder

There are many ways in which teachers can help their students manage their school year. One of the best is to teach them to organize their tasks into a manageable calendar of events. A section of the student's notebook or a separate spiral notebook may be used to keep a record of the assignments or tasks the student will perform on a daily basis. Some persons prefer a calendar book similar to a "Day at a Glance." Other teachers prefer to make a 10-month school calendar book for each of their students or reproduce a monthly page from a calendar. This book or pages can then be hole punched and kept in the student's notebook. Students can also be asked to purchase a calendar book as part of their school supplies in September.

Objective

to teach the students how to use a binder reminder, a first step to ingraining the essential life skill of effective use of one's time

Activities

All entries in the binder reminder should be on a daily basis. Parents should be encouraged to check their student's binders nightly for homework assignments and other important school-related activities.

Impress upon the students that the skills they learn by using the binder reminder provide life-long benefits, no matter what their future roles may be—athlete, homemaker, military, professional, businessperson, or tradesperson.

Daily Use

- Teachers should log the assignments into their own reminders in full view of the class.

- Allow a few minutes daily for the students to make their entries.

- Remind students to include due dates with their assignments.

- Have students record school holidays, special events, and other school-related activities directly into their reminders.

- Assign a "study buddy" or allow the students to pick another student to call if they are absent.

Binder Reminder

Instructions to the Student

- Enter all assignments in a consistent manner.

- Print or write all entries neatly and concisely.

- Update previously entered data relating to changed due dates, assignment requirements, and/or possible conflicts, as they become known.

- Maintain commitments to due dates.

- Establish priority listings for work that is due on a given day.

- Review entries on a daily basis to ensure all assignments are completed.

- Record personal and social information and commitments.

Name _____

School_____

Homeroom _____

Daily Assignment Reminder

Monday		Date
Math	Language Arts	Science
Social Studies	Foreign Language	Elective

Tuesday		Date
Math	Language Arts	Science
Social Studies	Foreign Language	Elective

Wednesday		Date
Math	Language Arts	Science
Social Studies	Foreign Language	Elective

Daily Assignment Reminder *(cont.)*

Thursday		Date
Math	Language Arts	Science
Social Studies	Foreign Language	Elective

Friday		Date
Math	Language Arts	Science
Social Studies	Foreign Language	Elective

Plan Ahead

List any future assignments or projects here.

Monthly Assignment Reminder

Month _____

Monday	Tuesday	Wednesday	Thursday	Friday

Time Management Award

presented to

_____

Signed _____

Date _____

Life Skills Vocabulary

Objective

to aid students to develop a strong concept of self and to provide the tools necessary for them to be successful

Materials

- construction paper, white and assorted colors
- glue stick
- markers

Activities

Reproduce the vocabulary list on this (or the following) page. Have the students prepare a "train of life" as shown in the diagram below. Use large colored construction paper for the individual cars. Cut out circles for the wheels. Print individual vocabulary words on the smaller white construction paper and mount one on each car. Connect the cars and display them in a chain around the room.

- **Integrity**
- **Initiative**
- **Flexibility**
- **Perseverance**
- **Organization**

- **Sense of Humor**
- **Effort**
- **Common Sense**
- **Problem Solving**
- **Responsibility**

- **Patience**
- **Friendship**
- **Curious**
- **Cooperation**
- **Caring**

Life Skills Vocabulary *(cont.)*

Complete the cars of the train by writing in your own words the definitions of the life skills vocabulary.

Accepting	Accommodating	Adaptable	Assertive
Busy	Beautiful	Brave	Calm
Caring	Cautious	Compassionate	Competent
Cheerful	Congenial	Considerate	Clear
Cooperative	Dedicated	Democratic	Discreet
Eager	Earnest	Enthusiastic	Energetic
Empathetic	Fair	Flexible	Friendly
Forgiving	Generous	Giving	Gracious
Humorous	Honest	Helpful	Independent
Imaginative	Inquisitive	Jovial	Just
Kind	Knowing	Leader	Liberal
Likeable	Lively	Logical	Loyal
Mathematical	Merry	Motivating	Mature
Mysterious	Nice	Noble	Natural
Objective	Organized	Optimistic	Open
Patient	Positive	Realistic	Reasonable
Reliable	Responsible	Refreshing	Receptive
Self-Confident	Sensitive	Sharing	Skillful
Sociable	Stable	Supportive	Tactful
Thoughtful	Trustworthy	Truthful	Unique
Understanding	Vigilant	Vital	Warm
Well-Balanced	Wise	Wholesome	Witty
Zealous	Zestful		

Life Skills Vocabulary *(cont.)*

1. Use the Life Skill Vocabulary words individually or in groups. Have each group define a word and draw a picture that would reflect what that word means.

2. In cooperative learning groups, have each group choose a life skill and write a skit that positively illustrates it (without saying the word).

   During the skits, each student has a Create-a-Skit Record sheet. After each skit, the students are to record the life skill that the skit shows.

   At the completion of all the skits, students are to meet with their cooperative groups and collectively decide on a final list. The correct answers are revealed, and a vote is taken for the best skit. This activity usually requires two periods.

4. After a weekend or a vacation, a student tells something that happened which favorably displays a life skill. The rest of the class guesses which life skill is illustrated. Incentives may be offered.

5. Have students create an advertisement for one of the life skills. Try a catchy jingle or phrase that will keep the life skill on everyone's mind.

Create-a-Skit Record Sheet

It is all right to look around the room at the life skill vocabulary words for a refresher on the skill that is being portrayed.

Group Number	Life Skill
1	
2	
3	
4	
5	
6	
7	
8	

Enter the names of your group members below.

_____   _____   _____

_____   _____

Enter the number of correct life skills you selected. [ ]

The Good Guy Award

presented to

Date

Signed

Compliments

Objective

to practice giving and receiving compliments to increase awareness of oneself

Materials

- a tennis ball or a ball small enough to be passed from student to student without detracting from the compliment

Activity

The students sit in a circle facing each other. The person given the tennis ball is the TALKER. The TALKER cites a life skill and the person who exhibits such behavior in the group. The TALKER then passes the ball to the person sitting on his/her right. That person now is the TALKER. This process continues until everyone has given and received a compliment.

Some students have difficulty giving and receiving compliments, but all will come away with good feelings about themselves and one another.

Examples

- *Patience*—David, I like the way you waited for Steven to finish speaking before you raised your hand.

- *Optimism*—It's nice to be around you, Karen, because you always look on the bright side of everything.

- *Maturity*—Well, Phil, the thing everybody likes about you is that you never act childish or selfish—you are well-balanced.

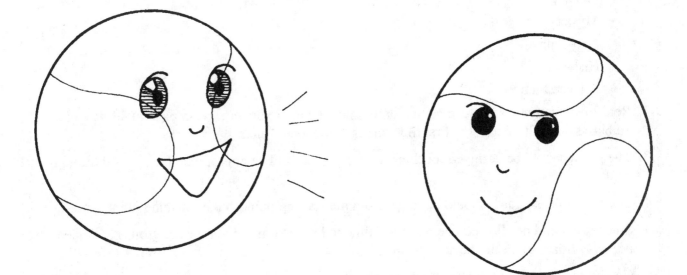

Design a Board Game

Objective

to create a game of life that is realistic and based on activities in students' own lives

(The teacher might want to have the Milton-Bradley game "Life" in the classroom to give students a visual example of what can be created. Other game boards may be provided to show various layouts.)

Materials for Each Group (ideally consisting of 4–5 members)

- tagboard or chipboard
- pencils
- rulers
- scissors
- matte knife (For safety, the teacher rather than the students should cut the chipboard or tagboard with a knife.)
- paste
- scratch paper
- assorted buttons, game pieces, spinners, etc.

Activity

1. Explain to the students that they are going to design a board game based on their lives.

2. They may choose any theme for their game.

   Examples might include the following:

   - Fantasy
   - Mystery
   - Geography
   - History
   - Science Fiction

3. Real-life situations (some can be humorous) may be incorporated. Examples might be a most embarrassing school day, the first time one is "grounded," etc.

3. The game should be designed for three to four players and be appropriate for ages 10 through adult.

4. The object of the game should be to get from the starting point to the finishing point.

5. Students should be allowed one period of time to brainstorm in their design groups and one to two periods of time to create the actual game.

6. Games can be kept in the classroom for the school year for the students to play in their free time.

52

Design-a-Game Team Planning Sheet

List the members of your design team.

1. _____

2. _____

3. _____

4. _____

5. _____

Name of Your Game _____

Theme of Your Game _____

Instructions for the design team _____

1. Design a board game for three to four players, ages 10 through adult.

2. You may choose any theme for your game. Some suggestions are history, fantasy, geography, science fiction, or mystery. Use your imagination. Be creative, but base it on the positive things in your lives.

   WARNING: Any team creating a game with any kind of violence will not receive credit for this activity.

3. Consider the following while creating your game:

   - lay-out of game board
   - chance cards
   - markers for the players
   - penalty and bonus moves
   - game rules
   - how the players move (spinners, dice, markers, etc.)
   - script for each space along the trail
   - art work and overall design of the game
   - making alternative routes to the finish
   - directions that are clear and easy to understand

4. Make a first draft of your game.

5. After your prototype is finished, play the game yourselves. Ask outsiders to test your game. Correct any defects.

6. Ask your design team these questions:

   - Is your game exciting to play?
   - Is it too easy?
   - Will others enjoy playing your game?
   - Can you make it better?

7. At this point, if your team feels the game is great, make your finished product!

Remember these elements: IMAGINATION . . . CREATIVITY . . . FUN!

The Imagination Award

presented to

_____

Date _____

Signed _____

Acknowledging Birthdays

Objective

to acknowledge birthdays in the classroom and accomplish three things:

- remind the students that they are special and unique
- build relationships among students
- build relationships between the student and teacher

Activities

It takes very little effort to acknowledge birthdays, and teachers will find the experience to be worthwhile.

☆ Put the student's name on a birthday calendar in the room.

☆ If a student's name is listed on a particular date, then that student gets a standing ovation.

☆ To acknowledge birthdays which fall in the summer months, give the student a **half-year birthday**.

☆ Make a birthday card on your computer for the student.

☆ Give a small candy treat (maybe raisins would be better).

☆ Print the names of your students' birthdays in your parent newsletter or add a **happy birthday** message on your Classlink or Homework Hotline.

☆ Sing a special birthday song:

Today, today, today, today, today is the day of your birthday!

Today, today, today, today, today is the day of your birthday.

It's not the flower's or the tree's, it's not the panda's or the bee's!

'Cause today, today, today, today,

Today is the day of YOUR birthday!

☆ Make a No Homework Birthday Pass (Middle school students enjoy this one more than any other. A birthday pass is provided on page 57.)

Birthday Calendar

Today, today, today, today, today is the day of your birthday!

September	March
_____ _____	_____ _____
_____ _____	_____ _____
_____ _____	_____ _____

October   **April**

November   **May**

December   **June**

January   **July**

February   **August**

No Homework Birthday Pass

Happy Birthday to_____!

Today is your birthday!

You may choose one homework assignment and skip it.

Signed_____

Happy Birthday to_____!

Today is your birthday!

You may choose one homework assignment and skip it.

Signed_____

It Just Bugs Me

Objective

to give students a place where they can vent irritations or anger

Materials

- scissors
- notebook paper
- pencils
- strips of white construction paper for the student to write what "bugs" him/her
- one 16" x 20" (40 cm x 50 cm) sheet of construction paper, assorted colors

Activity

(This activity can be used as a bulletin board display, a writing assignment, or as a complaint sheet in the student's notebook.)

Bulletin Board Display

1. Fold the sheet of construction paper in half lengthwise.

2. Using a pencil, write your name (first or last or both) in script with the bottom of the letters touching the fold.

3. Carefully cut around the letters of your name, but do not cut on the fold.

4. Open the paper and you have your own unique bug.

5. On the white strip, neatly write "It just bugs me when . . . " and add your pet peeve.

6. Arrange the bugs and peeves on a bulletin board.

Writing Assignment

1. Fold a sheet of notebook paper about one-third of the way down from the top.   Open the paper.

2. Write your name, in script, on the fold in pencil. Trace over the name a few times to make the pencil mark dark.

3. Fold the paper closed and rub the back of the fold and the name to make a mirror image of the name.

4. Make the rubbed impression darker by tracing over it, and you have your bug.

5. Discuss with the class how everyone is "bugged" by different things. You might even want to relate some of your peeves.

6. Use the lower third of the paper for the students to write about "What Bugs Me."

Notebook Page

This procedure is the same as for the writing assignment, but a list of peeves or bugs is kept in the students' notebooks.

As students encounter situations which bug them, they have a place to vent those feelings. See the following page for a "bug list."

It Just Bugs Me (cont.)

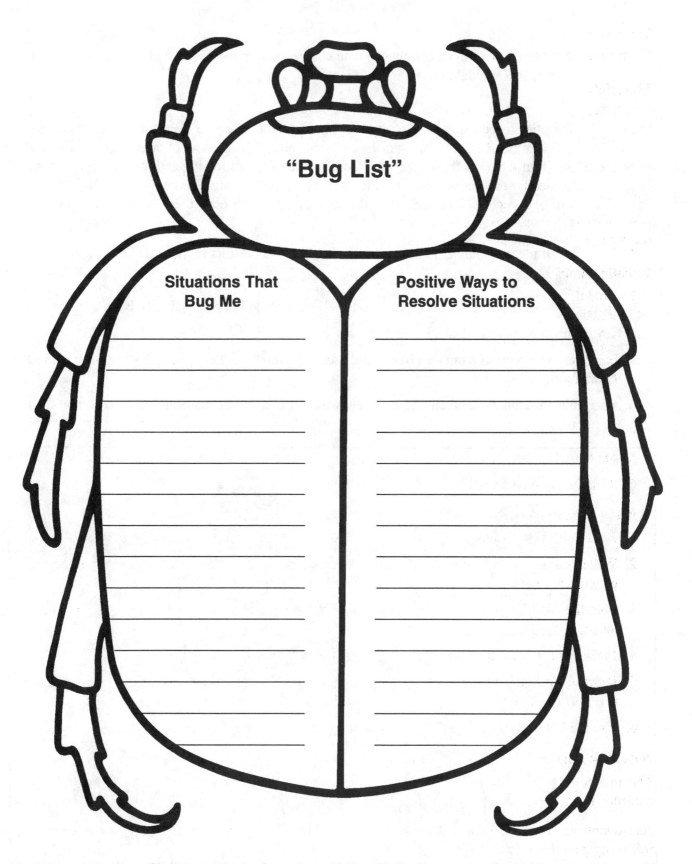

"Bug List"

Situations That Bug Me

Positive Ways to Resolve Situations

Becoming Test Wise

Objective

to improve students' comfort, confidence, and competence in meeting the challenge of multiple tests and teachers in middle school

Activities

The specific activities listed below relate to test-taking alone, but they are a part of the larger category of study skills which include time management and goal setting. There are, of course, some obviously overlapping areas among all of these elements. At any rate, if the following actions are regularly and sincerely performed by the teacher, the students cannot help benefitting. The mere regularity of presentation will help each student internalize the strategies and habituate them to positive test-taking behaviors.

1. Have your students evaluate how they study. Review their results individually or as a group.

2. Display large copies of Test-Taking Strategies in the room.

3. Make copies of the Test-Taking Strategies for all students to keep in their notebooks.

4. Review each one of the strategies with the students.

5. Continue to review the strategies before each test or quiz. This keeps the information fresh in the student's mind.

6. After your students have taken a test, review what mistakes were made and how to correct them for the next test.

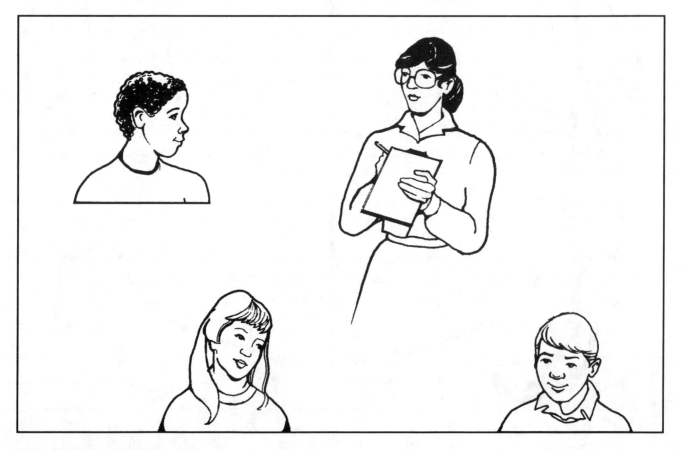

Becoming Test Wise (cont.)

Distribute the following questionnaire to the students and have them complete it.

1. Where do you study?

   _____

2. What conditions prevent you from studying? (Too hot or cold? Little brother or sister too noisy? Too late or too early in the day?)

   _____

   _____

3. Do you have all the materials necessary for the subject you are studying? (books, pencils, pens, erasers)

   _____

4. How can you limit distractions?

   _____

5. What do you think you can do to make better use of your study time?

   _____

   _____

6. How much time do you spend studying before a test?

   _____

7. Do you feel the amount of time you spend studying needs to be changed? Why or why not?

   _____

8. Do you study a little each day, or do you cram the night before the test?

   _____

9. Have you sometimes (or often) done your best to study and still done poorly on a test? If you answered yes, why do you think that is? If you answered no, what study methods did you use? Write them down so that you can use them on the next test.

   _____

   _____

10. Listen to the responses of your classmates and write down those study techniques that have worked for them and use them in your next study session.

    _____

    _____

    _____

How Do You Learn?

Objective

to help your students understand how they learn so that they can study for a test in the best manner for them

Activity

Have your students complete the Self-Analysis Study.

Have the students score the sheets and make entries about their particular study needs at the bottom of the page.

Instruct the students to refer to these guides the next time they study for a test.

Facts About Learning

- Once the students understand their individual styles of learning, they will be less apprehensive about taking tests, and the teacher is more likely to know how to meet their needs.

- A student's learning style is generally the same for any subject matter that he or she may study.

- Students learn best when they study while using their individual learning styles.

- Persistent and responsible students score higher on tests and achieve higher grades.

- The more a student can use a combination of learning modalities, the more permanent the information will become.

Self-Analysis Study

Circle your response to the questions.

1. Do you need a quiet place to study?   yes   no

2. Do you study in a well-lighted place?   yes   no

3. Are you aware of room temperature when you study?   yes   no

4. Do you schedule a special time for daily study?   yes   no

5. Do you need to move when you are studying?   yes   no

6. Do you study late in the day?   yes   no

7. Do you study early in the day?   yes   no

8. Is your study too structured?   yes   no

9. Are you motivated to study on your own?   yes   no

10. Can you work on task for 45 minutes?   yes   no

11. Do you learn best by yourself?   yes   no

12. Do you learn best by reading and seeing?   yes   no

13. Do you learn best by hearing?   yes   no

14. Do you learn best by doing?   yes   no

15. Do you learn best by saying?   yes   no

16. Do you learn best when you are hungry?   yes   no

17. Do you learn best on a full stomach?   yes   no

18. Do you need absolute quiet to do well?   yes   no

19. Do you need to hear quiet music to study?   yes   no

20 Do you schedule enough time to complete your studying? yes   no

Total number of "yes" answers   [   ]

Total number of "no" answers   [   ]

Self-Analysis Study *(cont.)*

List all the "yes" questions that tell you how you study best. Make them a part of your study routine.

_____

_____

_____

_____

_____

_____

List all the questions to which you answered "no." Avoid these roadblocks to good learning.

_____

_____

_____

_____

_____

_____

_____

_____

Answer the following questions about how you study.

- What did you learn about how you study?

  _____

- What do you think about your style of learning?

  _____

- After learning that you have certain favorable styles of learning, are you going to change what you have been doing?_____

- How will you make the changes? _____

- Do you make excuses for not studying? What are they? _____

- Can you expect to do well if you continue to make excuses? _____

Review the results of this survey with your parents. They can help you by providing the requirements you need to study and work to the best of your ability.

Test-Taking Strategies—Before Testing

1. Find a quiet place and assemble all the materials you will need to study for your test.

   - notes
   - books
   - pens and pencils

   - paper
   - snack
   - 3" x 5" (7.5 cm x 12.5 cm) index cards

2. Before you begin, make certain that your notes and study materials are complete. Call a friend if you have been absent and double check to be sure.

3. Form a study group. Other people provide the opportunity to practice and review.

4. Let's begin:

   a. Divide material into what you know well, what you need to review, and what is unfamiliar to you.

   b. Use index cards to record the following:

      - vocabulary
      - definitions
      - spelling words

      - formulas
      - lists of cause and effects
      - summaries of concepts or catch phrases for concepts

   c. Review the material you know well.

   d. Focus on material that you need to review and spend enough time in this area to become confident about your knowledge of the material.

   e. Unfamiliar material will need the most study time. Begin to study this material a few days before the test.

      - Outline the chapters.
      - Make note cards.
      - Look up unfamiliar words.

      - Turn chapter headings into sub-headings.
      - Organize notes and materials.

5. The evening before a test should be spent reviewing all your material.

6. Test yourself and re-study any weak areas.

7. Get a good night's rest and do not forget to eat a good healthy breakfast.

Test-Taking Strategies—Day of Testing

1. Bring the proper materials to the test with you.

   - two sharpened pencils
   - two pens
   - any other allowable materials needed for this particular test—calculator, scientific tables, mathematical materials, etc.

2. Arrive at class a few minutes early. Settle in and get comfortable.

3. Do not talk to others about test material. This can only confuse you.

4. Put your name on all pages of the test.

5. Look over the complete test before answering any of the questions

6. Think positive thoughts. Make an effort to relax your neck, shoulders, and upper back.

7. Read all the directions carefully. Directions can be tricky.

   - Are you supposed to circle the correct word, underline it, or write it in the margins?
   - Are your answers supposed to be written in complete sentences? Should you write on the test paper or on a separate sheet of paper? Do you understand how to bubble in a machine scored test?

8. Keep your mind on the test.

9. Read all the questions before you read the story.

10. On multiple choice tests, read all the answers.

11. Pace yourself. Do not spend a lot of time on a question you do not know. You can go back after you have finished the test.

12. Work on one question at a time.

13. Do not worry about the pace of other classmates. Keep a pace that is good for your completion of the test.

14. Use intelligent guessing when you do not know the answer to a question.

15. Never change an answer unless it is clearly wrong.

16. If you have time left over at the end of a test, review your answers, but do not forget rule 15.

Good luck!

Test-Taking Strategies—After Testing

Although most students would like to forget tests once they are completed and returned, much can be learned from them.

When tests are returned, even if you did well, you should always review them. Why?

1. Learn to avoid repeating mistakes.

2. Read the grader's comments.
   - Turn any criticism into a tool for future tests.
   - Learn from your mistakes.
   - Make a mental note of what you did well and try to do it again.

3. Look for specifics.
   - What kinds of questions did you answer well?
   - What kinds of questions did you do poorly on and why? Teachers are more than willing to help their students improve in answering questions.
   - Was something missing from your notes?
   - What can you do differently the next time you have a test?

4. Keep a file of your tests for future reference. This will refresh your memory on the kinds of questions your teacher asks.

5. Get help from family, friends, and (most importantly) your teacher when you do poorly. They are your best supporters.

6. Do not agonize about a poor test. It will make you anxious, uncertain, and apprehensive the next time you take a test.

Organizing Study Materials

Objective

to help students gain the ability to organize, identify, and create study notes for a chapter, lesson, or reading material needed for a test

Materials

- pen or pencil

- material to organize—any lesson, chapter, or reading material from any subject area

- notebook paper for each student

Activity

1. Using notebook paper and a pencil, ask the students to draw a large "T" on their notebook paper. (A model is provided on the following page.) Note the vertical bar is slightly to the left of center.

2. As students use this sheet of paper and any succeeding sheets, have them remember the following:

   a. Put their names on each page—preferably in the upper right hand corner.

   b. Date each page—preferably at the top of the page in the middle of the top margin.

   c. Number each page—in the upper right hand margin

   d. Place the chapter title on the horizontal line of the "T."

   e. Write the main ideas of the material to the left of the vertical bar.—These are often the bold-face-print points of information.

   f. Write details or supporting facts of information to the right of the vertical bar as shown in the example.

Closure

Teachers should check that the students are doing this procedure correctly the first few times they do notes. It does not take long for the students to learn this study method.

Suggestions

- Leave plenty of margin space. This allows for the addition of any information found from other sources.

- Write in notes or phrases. It is not necessary to use full sentences.

- When studying, students can fold their papers along the vertical "T" line and study either main points or details.

- Keep study sheets in binders. Then they are in a convenient place to find them when needed.

Correct Note-Taking Form

Name of Topic

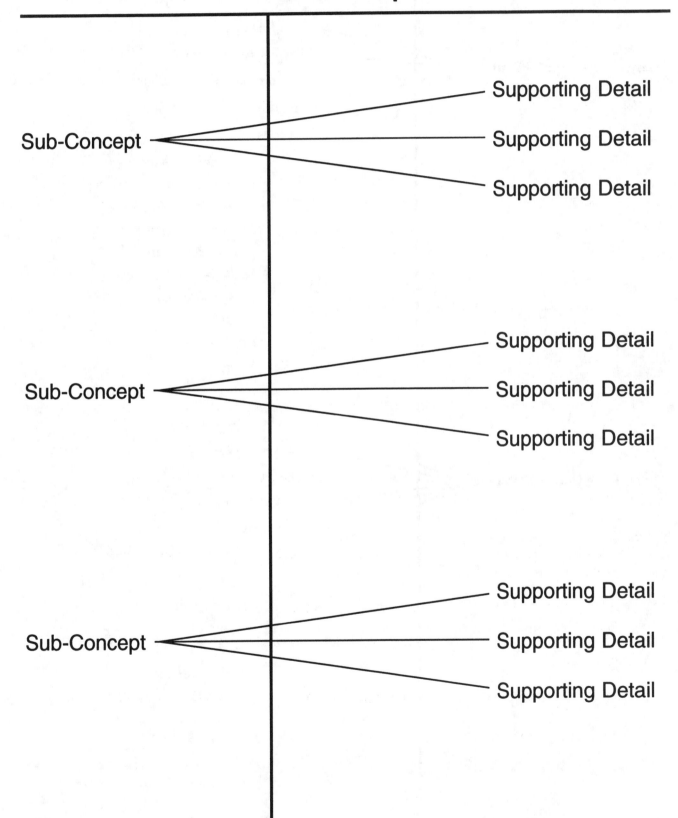

Sub-Concept — Supporting Detail
Supporting Detail
Supporting Detail

Sub-Concept — Supporting Detail
Supporting Detail
Supporting Detail

Sub-Concept — Supporting Detail
Supporting Detail
Supporting Detail

Sample T-Diagram

Dogs

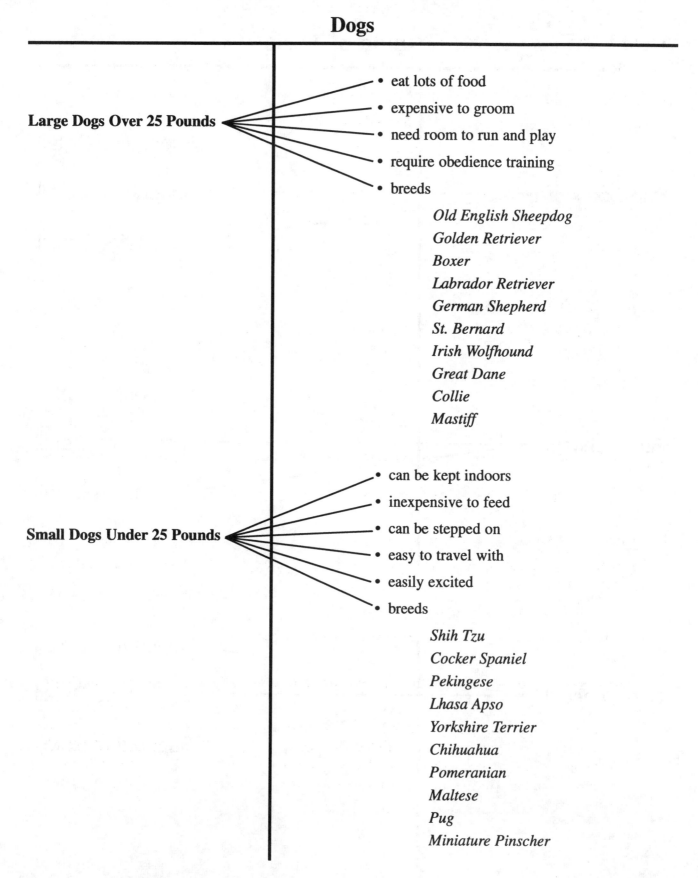

Large Dogs Over 25 Pounds

- eat lots of food
- expensive to groom
- need room to run and play
- require obedience training
- breeds

  Old English Sheepdog
  Golden Retriever
  Boxer
  Labrador Retriever
  German Shepherd
  St. Bernard
  Irish Wolfhound
  Great Dane
  Collie
  Mastiff

Small Dogs Under 25 Pounds

- can be kept indoors
- inexpensive to feed
- can be stepped on
- easy to travel with
- easily excited
- breeds

  Shih Tzu
  Cocker Spaniel
  Pekingese
  Lhasa Apso
  Yorkshire Terrier
  Chihuahua
  Pomeranian
  Maltese
  Pug
  Miniature Pinscher

Tips for Test Taking

Remember: You have studied hard and you know your material, so relax!

- Read through the entire test before you begin to write.

- Be alert to negative words in questions, especially double negatives. They tend to trick you.

- Do not waste time on questions you do not know. Go back to them at the end of the test.

- Never change an answer unless it is clearly wrong.

- Ignore the pace of your fellow students. Just because they are finished, does not mean they have done well.

- Sometimes a question or an answer will trigger the recalling of another answer.

- Take the test with a positive attitude. Thinking positively can keep you calm and cool.

- Be test wise. To help you do your best, use the hints that follow for specific types of tests.

- Above all . . . put your name on all the pages of your test.

Hints for Multiple Choice Tests

Most students seem to prefer multiple choice tests because they feel that even if they do not know the answer, they have a good chance of getting the question right through a logical pattern of steps.

You can too if you follow these simple steps.

1. Read the question carefully. Then read the question again with each of the given choices. Choose the answer that makes the most complete thought or the most sense.

2. Still not sure of the answer? Then eliminate the extremes. Look for the the answers that make no sense and throw them out. That leaves you two answers to choose from, and it is less intimidating to have two rather than four or five choices. Choose the best of the two for your answer.

3. Statements such as *all of the above* are usually correct answers.

4. Many times the answer with the most details is the best choice. Most test writers would not put that much effort into a wrong answer.

5. If two of your choices are opposite, choose one of them.

6. If two of the choices are close in their meaning or are nearly saying the same thing, choose neither one.

7. An answer is probably right if it is in the middle of the choices, especially if it is a long answer.

8. It is important to remember that no answer is just as bad as a wrong answer, so if all else fails make your best guess. The Princeton Review, a preparation course for the SATs, suggests that you pick letter B if you have no clue to the right answer. They seem to feel that most test writers would not put the answer in the first or the last position, and of the remaining two, B seems to be the most common. However . . . it is always more important to study than to guess!

Tips for Test Taking *(cont.)*

Hints for True/False Tests

These are the most difficult types of test to take. They are so difficult because the answer is either right or wrong, and there is no real way to eliminate some answers. However, there are still some things you can do.

1. Read all the questions twice. Again there may be some triggers to the right answer in some of the questions.
2. Do NOT analyze the question for a deeper meaning. Read it for what is written, not what you think the questions means.
3. If you must guess, answer *true* because the odds are better. Hint: There are usually more true answers than false answers because they are easier to write.
4. Simplify the question into smaller sections. Simplicity is easier to understand.
5. Keep your teacher's point of view in mind when you answer the question. In other words, what would your teacher answer?
6. Answer *false* if any part of the statement is incorrect.
7. Statements with reasons or incomplete reasons are usually false.

Hints for Fill-in-the-Blank Tests

1. Look for clue words such as *a, an, the, these, those,* and *they.* They can signal the proper agreement with the nouns.
2. If you cannot think of the correct word, think of one that is similar or closely related to the answer.
3. Be sure the answer you write makes sense in the statement. Teachers tend to take statements directly from the text.
4. Look for the verb in the sentence. Sometimes the verb can give clues to the type of answer you need to write.
5. Do not leave any blanks. A guess may be worth partial credit. It is better than no credit at all.

Hints for Essay Tests

1. Read the questions carefully. Write down key words and phrases that come to mind when you read the questions.
2. Organize your key words into complete thoughts and add details.
3. Budget your time. Partial credit for incomplete answers is better than no credit for questions not attempted.
4. Answer your questions as if you were writing a story. Begin with a good topic sentence, add supporting details, and write a good conclusion.
5. Review what you have written. Check for spelling errors, grammatical mistakes, content, and organization.
6. Do not ramble. Make sure your answers reflect what the question is asking.
7. Be sure you say what you mean to say!

Tips for Test Taking *(cont.)*

Hints for Open Book Tests

Open book tests require some prior preparation. Just because you can use a book, do not think that the test will be a breeze. You still need to study and be famililar with the information that is in your textbook.

1. Before the test day, reread your test information. Become familiar with the vocabulary and the content that you will be tested on.

2. On index cards, write important facts and page numbers where you can find specific facts if you are allowed to bring them to the testing room. CHECK WITH YOUR TEACHER PRIOR TO THE TEST DAY.

3. Read the chapters that you are being tested on. Become knowledgeable about the charts, graphs, and tables that are in your book.

4. Read the entire test before you begin to write. Once again, you will be able to make judgments about how you need to plan your time and what test-taking strategies you can use.

5. Scan the test for the types of questions that appear. Remember that essay questions take longer to answer than other types.

Hints for Take-Home Tests

These are probably the simplest of all the different types of tests, but do not become lax about your pre-test preparation.

1. Read the test before you leave school and make a list of all the materials you need to take home with you. There is nothing worse than not being able to get to your books because you left them in your locker.

2. Read the directions. Ask any questions you may have about what you are supposed to do.

3. Find out if the test is to be completed individually or in groups.

4. Be clear about the day and time the test is due.

5. At home find a place where you will be able to complete your test without any interruptions.

6. Assemble all the materials you might need to use on your test and BEGIN!

7. Plan and organize your answers.

8. Do not copy directly from your book unless you quote the material.

9. Attach a list of the references you used to your test paper. This will allow your teachers a source to verify what you have written if they are unclear about what you said. Remember that teachers are human and really do not know everything!

10. When you are finished, write your name on all your pages and staple them together. Put your test in a safe place until you are ready to hand in your paper.

Tips for Research Papers

Objective

to provide students a guide for writing proper research papers or other types of formal writing

Activity

1. Copy the Research Paper Guide Sheet for each of your students.

2. The students should be instructed to keep this sheet in their binders for reference throughout the school year.

3. Discuss the material found on the guide sheet with your students for full understanding.

4. Copy the Evaluation Sheet for each of your students.

5. Review how you will be grading their work and what you expect from them. Points may be given instead of letter grades.

6. Remember this is only a guide for research papers. There are many other ways that you might want your class to complete them. Please feel free to adapt this form to suit your individual students' needs.

ALWAYS TRY TO KEEP GRADING IN THE SAME FORMAT FOR ALL THE STUDENT WORK. (This eliminates constantly explaining grades to the students.)

Research Paper Guide Sheet

I. **Select a specific subject and appropriate topic.**

    A. Write the name of your topic on a 3" x 5" (7.5 cm x 12.5 cm) index card.

    B. Get your topic approved by your teacher.

II. **Think of at least five things you want to learn.**

    A. List these things on the back of your index card.

    B. Get your sub-topics approved by your teacher.

III. **Begin researching your topic. Use a variety of sources such as books, magazines, encyclopedias, interviews, and videos.**

    A. Take notes from each of these research resources.

    B. Use a different sheet of paper for your notes from each of the sources.

    C. At the top of each page of notes, include the information you will need for your bibliography.

    D. Get your notes approved by your teacher.

IV. **Write the body of your report.** Make sure you write using your own notes. DO NOT COPY DIRECTLY FROM YOUR RESOURCE! If you write from your notes, you will avoid stealing other people's words, which is against the law.

    A. Remember to write your paper using the third person point of view. That means do not use *I, me,* or *we.*

    B. Give the facts. Be sure to leave your feelings and opinions out of your paper.

    C. Stick to the topic of your research. Have lots of support paragraphs to prove and explain your topic.

    D. This is a rough draft. Be sure to read it through and correct all errors. Then have two other people proofread your rough draft too!

    E. Get your rough draft approved by your teacher.

V. **Assemble your research report.**

    A. COVER (5 Points) It can be a ready-made folder, or it can be made from construction paper. On the folder have the title, your name, date, and period or class.

    B. TITLE PAGE (10 Points) The title page should have your title, your name, and some type of appropriate graphic.

    C. TABLE OF CONTENTS (10 Points) A table of contents needs a title, subtitles, page numbers, and some type of graphic.

    D. BODY OF THE REPORT (50 Points) Your report must be typed or written in black ink. Copy your rough draft carefully.

    E. APPENDIX (15 Points) The appendix can include a lot of things. It is made of any additional materials that would make your report interesting. It could include charts, drawings, pictures, photographs, maps, diagrams, a newspaper article, poems, a glossary, etc.

    F. BIBLIOGRAPHY (10 Points) Your bibliography needs a title, an alphabetical list of all resources, and some appropriate graphics for decoration.

NOTE: You need to plan your time wisely. Points will be deducted for each day your paper is late.

Research Report Evaluation Sheet

Name: _____ Date: _____

EXPLANATION OF MARKS:

O = Outstanding

S = Satisfactory

AC = Area of Concern

CONTENT

_____ Title

_____ Introduction

_____ Supporting Paragraphs

_____ Writes to Topic

_____ Includes Many Details

_____ Conclusion

MECHANICS

_____ Capitalization

_____ End Punctuation

_____ Spelling

_____ Grammar/Usage

_____ Sentence Structure

_____ Paragraph Indentation

_____ Margins

_____ General Punctuation

CREATIVITY

_____ Appropriate Title

_____ Has Interesting Graphics

_____ Uses Varied Vocabulary

_____ Uses Variety in Sentences

PARTS OF THE REPORT	POSSIBLE POINTS	YOUR TOTAL SCORE
a. Cover	5	_____
b. Title Page	10	_____
c. Table of Contents	10	_____
d. Body of the Report	50	_____
e. Appendix	15	_____
f. Bibliography	10	_____

TOTAL POSSIBLE POINTS = 100   **YOUR TOTAL POINTS** _____

YOUR GRADE _____

The Inquiring Mind Award

presented to

_____

Signed _____

Date _____

Getting Ready for Second Quarter

Objective

to allow the student time to reflect and recall what went well and what did not during the first quarter

(Some students are slow in getting started after a long summer vacation, and some self-reflection makes them aware of what they need to do during the second quarter.)

Activity

1. Enlarge the following page. You might also want to copy one for each of your students. Tell them that nearly all people want to be the best that they can be, but some people just do not try hard enough.

2. Encourage a discussion in class as to what it takes to be the best that you can be. Some students might say that if they had money they could be anything they wanted. Ask: " What about persons who have handicaps? What does it mean for them to be the best that they can be?" Bring up other physical limitations. At this point your students should be volunteering information on various limitations that some people have to overcome.

3. Distribute the questionnaire that follows the chart and ask your students to complete it.

4. When they have finished, collect the pages and distribute them to other students for suggestions on how that person might achieve his/her goals. For those who are too embarrassed, the teacher can collect their papers and offer some personal suggestions.

Closure

Although self-assessment is an on-going process, this activity can produce a listing of ways that the class can implement to improve themselves.

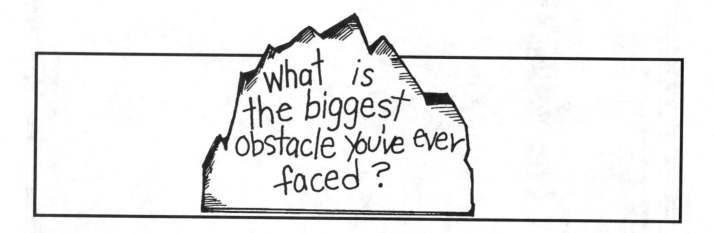

To be the best you can be, ask yourself . . .

Is it safe?

Is it respectful?

Is it responsible?

Is it considerate?

Is it cooperative?

If any answer is no, be proud of yourself—don't do it!

First Quarter Student Survey

Name_____ Date _____

Answer the following questions as honestly as you can.

1. Think about the events of the first quarter. How did the start of the school year feel to you?

   _____

2. Did you feel that you were the best that you could be? _____

3. What things or events do you feel were successful for you?

   _____

4. What things or events were a disaster?

   _____

5. If you could start the school year over again, what changes would you make?

   _____

6. How might those changes have helped you to be more successful?

   _____

7. Can any of those changes be implemented in the second quarter?_____

8. What things can you do to be successful?_____

9. How can your classmates help you be successful?

   _____

10. Is there anything your teacher can do to make you more successful? ("No homework!" is an unacceptable answer.) _____

11. What do you think has hindered you from becoming more successful?

    _____

12. Have you put forth your greatest effort? Be Honest!_____

13. What improvements can you make in the second quarter?

    _____

14. If you make a bigger effort, do you think you will be more successful? Why or why not?

    _____

Complete the next question after your classmates have made some helpful suggestions to you.

15. Do you feel that the suggestions offered might be able to help you be the best? Why or why not?

    _____

    _____

List the suggestions your classmates made and explain how you might implement them in the second quarter.

Write Your Epitaph

Objective

to have students express their concepts of themselves by writing original epitaphs

Activity

An epitaph is a short statement written on a tomb in memory of the person buried there. Epitaphs often portray the buried person as good and loving. In this activity students will be given the opportunity to reflect on the persons they would like the world to remember them as. Epitaphs do not have to rhyme, but it is fun if they do.

This is a good activity to use at Halloween. It fits the feeling of the holiday.

1. Before beginning this activity, give the students the definition of *epitaph.*

One dictionary defines an epitaph as an inscription on or at a tomb in memory of the one buried there; or a brief statement worded as if to be inscribed on a monument.

2. Explain to the class the three most important things about epitaphs.

   a. They record the continuity of life.

   b. They tell us the importance of that person in society.

   c. They reflect the role that person played in relation to others.

3. Have the students find epitaphs in books of poetry. Some begin "There was an old man. . . , etc."

4. Mount the epitaphs on tombstones cut from black construction paper.

Variations

There are many curious and funny epitaphs. Have your students find some and recite them to the class.

1. Visit a local cemetery and make some gravestone rubbings. Find as much information as you can about one person buried there. When you select the name of a person, pretend you were that person and write the answers to the following questions.

   a. Who was I?

   b. Where did I live?

   c. How old was I?

   d. Did I have a family?

   e. What was my profession?

   f. What were my hobbies?

2. Tell the students that they are going to write their own epitaphs on the "My Own Epitaph" sheet. Remind them to reflect on a part of their lives for which they would like to be remembered.

Sample Epitaphs

Sonny

1963–1995

Here lies our dear, rich friend Sonny,

who died penniless

'cause she spent all her money!

R. I. P.

Here lies teenager Joan,

who starved to death

talking on the phone!

Jonathan Sturk

Farewell to Jonathan Sturk,

who's finally free from

doing his homework!

Mrs. Crouch

Here lies old Mrs. Crouch

whose kids didn't like her

'cause she was a grouch!

Resources for Students

1. Beable, W. H. *Epitaphs.* Thomas Y. Crowell Company, 1971.
2. Brown, Raymond L. *A Book of Epitaphs.* Taplinger Publishing Company, 1969.
3. Mann, Thomas C. and Janet Greene. *Over Their Dead Bodies.* The Steven Greene Press, 1962.
4. Wallis, Charles, L. *Stories on Stone.* Oxford University Press, 1954.

My Own Epitaph

Draw your own tombstone and compose your personal epitaph, remembering to reflect on that part of your life for which you would most like to be remembered.

Second Quarter

Life Skills Dealing with Emotion

Study Skills

- Being a Good Listener
- Identifying Learning Styles
- Identifying Thinking Styles

Goal Setting

My Problem Is . . .

Objective

to allow students to express problems they are concerned with and to explore possible solutions

Materials Needed for the Class

- box (A shoe box with a lid is appropriate, but any box will do.)
- 3" x 5" (7.5 cm x 12.5 cm) index cards
- pen or pencil

Activity

- Keep a "Dear Abby" box—allow students to put in problems or any other topic they wish to discuss anytime they have one.
- Explain to the class that problems often occur during times when they cannot be addressed and that the "Dear Abby" box is a great place to write down their problems for future discussion and resolution from the class.
- Students are requested to write their concerns on a piece of paper and drop it into the box. Explain that names are not necessary and it is up to the teacher to choose which problems are open to class discussion.
- Further explain that the students may place personal problems in the box, but they require names and that the students and teacher will meet privately to discuss the problem.
- By providing a safe environment for the students to vent their concerns, many petty squabbles can be avoided, thereby lessening other means of conflict.
- Prior to addressing the problems, the teacher should review the problems in the "Dear Abby" box to rule out any that are unsuitable for general discussion. Then the more common ones can be presented for discussion.
- Spend one day a week addressing the problems in the box. It is very important that this be an ongoing classroom activity and that problems are handled in a discreet and nonthreatening manner.
- Choose a problem for the box and allow the students to offer possible solutions. When you feel the students have exhausted their ideas, then you can offer some solutions.

Procedure

1. Explain to the students that sometimes everyone needs help with their problems. Sometimes there occur problems with which we need immediate help, and sometimes we can wait. The best place to get help with your problems is with parents, but they are not always available or your problem is school-related and maybe parents cannot help.
2. Display the "Dear Abby" box and explain the purpose to the students.
3. Tell the students that anytime a problem occurs that they would like to share, they should jot it down and place it in the box. Then once a week—Friday afternoon is a usually a good time—the class will discuss the problem and see if we can come up with some solutions.
4. It is all right to include problems one may have with one's friends, for someone else might also have the same problem.

Do not expect to see problems every week; some weeks are just perfect!

I've Got a Problem!

• What is your problem?

_____

_____

_____

_____

• How have you tried to solve this problem on your own?

_____

_____

_____

• Who have you discussed this problem with?

_____

_____

_____

• What suggestions did those people make?

_____

_____

_____

• Name (optional)

_____

• Would you like a private conference with the teacher?

_____

Treasure Hunt

Objective
to allow the student time to reflect on what makes him/her special

Materials
- typing paper
- pen or pencil

Activity
1. Tell your students that each one of us has some buried treasure inside us. Every one of us has some unique qualities that make us special.

2. Today, we are going to share some of those qualities. Instruct the students to think about themselves—who they are and what makes them distinct from everyone else in the class.

3. Distribute the paper to your students. Ask them to write or draw a picture of something that they feel is special about themselves. Have your students share their special qualities with each other. They may be surprised to find that no two of them are alike.

4. Have your students choose someone else in the class and do the same thing for them—that is, write or draw a picture of something special about that person. Then share the results. Being complimented is always a "feel good" situation.

All About Me!

Objective

first, to give the students a chance to reflect on what they are today and second, to compare their growth over the school year

Materials

- an "All About Me" survey sheet

- clear tape

- a shoe box decorated to resemble a treasure chest

- a large tape measure for accurate measurements of students' bodies

Activity

1. Copy the time capsule activity sheet (page 89), one per student.

2. Distribute the time capsule activity sheets and explain to your students that today they are going to describe themselves physically.

3. Discuss what physical attributes are and how they differ from person to person.

4. Explain that at this age their bodies are rapidly changing but that they sometimes may not be aware of this because, although rapid, such changes are gradual—not sudden.

5. Explain that by completing this activity they will have an exact way to see how they have changed in just this school year.

6. Then near the end of the year they will get this sheet back and complete the second part. At that time, discuss how everyone has changed.

   Note: Some students (particularly girls) may be acutely aware of and self-conscious about bodily changes at this age. Public discussion or attention focusing on them may cause substantial embarrassment; thus it is necessary that the teacher show great care and sensitivity in this activity. As is well-documented, weight alone can be a subject of acute worry to some students.

7. When all the time capsule sheets are completed, collect them and put them in a safe place for the future. A folder in your filing cabinet, a drawer in your desk, or designated space on a bookshelf might be good places. It is important to remember where you put them and to make a note in your plan book or calendar that you will use them in early June.

All About Me! *(cont.)*

A "time capsule" is a container that holds historical records. This survey is a time capsule about you, and you are the only one who will see it. Fill in the first set of blanks for each item below. When you are finished, fold your survey in thirds and seal it with clear tape. Write your name on the front of the folded sheet and give it to your teacher for safe keeping until June when you will be given the opportunity to compare how you have changed. You may be as honest as you wish since you will be the only one to see this survey.

Name_____	Date_____	Date_____
My height:	____ft. ____in. ____cm.	____ft. ____in. ____cm.
My weight:	____lbs. ____kg.	____lbs. ____kg.
The things I worry about most:		
The persons I most admire:		
My best friend:		
My favorite foods:		
My favorite songs:		
My favorite game:		
My favorite color:		
My favorite TV program:		
When grown, I want to be:		
The latest thing I have learned in math:		
My newest friends:		
The thing I want most:		
The last time I was really scared:		

Understanding Myself

Objective
to allow the students to examine the limits they put on doing things for others

Materials
- a list of the "Would You?" questions for each group leader
- paper and pencil for each group member, including the group leader

Activity

1. Explain to the class that most people would do more for a friend than they would do for a stranger. In some cases one might do more for a friend than a brother or a sister. However, we also have limits as to how much we will do for anyone. By doing the following activity, students will have an opportunity to look at just how much we would do for other people.

2. Divide the students into small groups and assign a group leader. Explain that the leader's responsibility in the group is to orally read the list of "Would You?" questions.

3. Give your students the following directions:

The group leader is going to read a list of "Would You?" questions, one at a time. Each of you is to answer "yes" or "no" to each question. Do not share your answers with each other or have any discussions among group members. There will be a group discussion after all the groups are finished.

4. Allow approximately 20 minutes for this part of the activity.

5. When the questions have been completed, instruct the students to count the number of NO responses and the number of YES responses.

Discussion
Ask the following questions of your students.

1. If I had a lot of NO answers, do I think I put too many restrictions on my friendships?

2. If I had a lot of YES responses, do I think I am too much of a "pushover" with my friends?

3. Am I happy with the limits I put on my friendship?

4. What changes might I make to ensure more successful relationships?

5. Would I tell my friends what I learned about myself and my friendships with others? Would it be helpful to let my friends know what I learned? Why or why not?

"Would You?"

Instructions to the Group Leader:

Read the questions one at a time and allow the members of your group sufficient time to think about the answers for a few moments.

WOULD YOU . . .

1. Give your friend your lunch money even if it means you will go without lunch?

2. Let a friend copy your paper and get credit for your idea?

3. Take the blame for a friend who has taken someone's money?

4. Remain friends with someone who has stolen your boyfriend or girlfriend?

5. Lend your friend your bike, even if you know no one else is supposed to ride it?

6. Lend your allowance to a friend, even if he or she will not tell you why it is wanted?

7. Let a friend drink from your soda can, even if he or she has just recovered from the flu?

8. Stop being friends with someone who turns you in for talking in class?

9. Stop being friends with someone who borrows a book from you, loses it, and shows no concern?

10. Continue to buy presents for a friend who never buys you a gift, even though you know that person can afford it?

11. Tell a friend who gives you a present that you do not like it?

12. Tell a very sensitive friend that he/she has bad breath?

    You may add questions of your own, but have them ready before starting the group discussion.

What I Am Not . . .

Objective

to give the students an opportunity to voice their views of themselves as compared to how they believe others see them

Activity

Reproduce and distribute the activity on this page for your students. Ask them to give some thought to the subject before they begin to write.

Follow Up

Allow several students to share their thoughts. Elicit discussion on why they feel that way and what misconceptions they might have about themselves. Try to encourage the students to be positive in their statements and try to end the discussion on a good note.

What I Am Not . . .

Complete the statement below and write a paragraph that explains why you feel that way. If you could change other people's opinions of you, what would you want them to think? How might you go about changing their opinions? Include the answers to these two questions in your paragraph of explanation.

Most people think I am_____

_____

_____

_____

_____

_____,

but I am really_____

_____

_____

_____

_____

_____

_____.

Can I Do Better Next Time?

Objective

to allow students to examine their methods of conflict resolution to see if there might be better ways to handle certain events that have happened in their lives

Activity

- Distribute the Reflection Activity Sheets to your students and allow time for the students to complete them. Make sure you allow time enough time for your students not to feel rushed. Usually 20 minutes is sufficient.

- Explain to the students that they are to reflect on the times when they wish they might have handled a situation better or they might have said something a little more diplomatically.

- Tell them to briefly describe those situations on the Reflection Activity Sheets and explain what they said or did.

- Then they are to reflect further and describe how they might now handle the situation differently if given the chance.

- Then have them choose one situation that they would like to discuss in class. Have the student read the situation to the class and then allow time for the class to suggest how it might be solved. Then have the student read how he or she solved it.

- Conclude with the class choosing the best way to handle further situations like these. This discussion provides for others to voice alternate suggestions about how each situation might have been handled better.

Name _____ Date _____

Reflection Activity Sheet

Situation 1

I remember the time . . .

_____

_____

_____

This is what happened . . .

_____

_____

_____

This is how I might do it differently if I could do it again . . .

_____

_____

_____

_____

_____

_____

Situation 2

I remember the time . . .

_____

_____

_____

This is what happened . . .

_____

_____

_____

This is how I might do it differently if I could do it again . . .

_____

_____

_____

_____

_____

_____

I Have the Right to Feel Good About Myself

Objective

Students at the middle school age often feel the need to be part of a group. They enjoy having friends around them who make them feel good. But even though they desire to be part of a group, at the same time they still need to feel special and unique. At this time parents and peers often become critical, and this criticism may lead the student to thoughts of inadequacy. A focus on positive qualities can be most helpful for students. It has been found that students who have positive self-esteem and can verbalize their strengths develop higher self-concepts and experience less anxiety and fewer failures.

This activity is intended to help the students focus on their strengths.

Activity

1. Provide the students with the list of descriptive words on the next page or modify the list to reflect the needs of your students.

2. Ask the students to select 5–10 words that reflect a quality about themselves.

3. Have the students write statements or paragraphs explaining why each word was selected and why that quality is important to them. Students may even choose to write an anecdotal situation depicting each word.

Variations

1. Use a tape recorder and have the students record their responses to the above lessons.

2. Videotaped anecdotes may be recorded with student permission and cooperation.

3. Students may elect to work in groups or pairs to complete this activity.

Caution:

Students should be allowed to work with those peers with whom they feel most comfortable. The teacher should not attempt to assign groups or share responses with the class unless the student gives his or her permission.

I Have the Right to Feel Good About Myself *(cont.)*

Word List

Accepting	Giving	Optimistic
Accommodating	Gracious	Patient
Adaptable	Helpful	Positive
Assertive	Honest	Realistic
Busy	Humorous	Reasonable
Beautiful	Imaginative	Receptive
Brave	Independent	Refreshing
Calm	Inquisitive	Reliable
Caring	Jovial	Responsible
Cautious	Just	Self-Confident
Cheerful	Kind	Sensitive
Clear	Knowing	Sharing
Compassionate	Leader	Skillful
Competent	Liberal	Sociable
Congenial	Likeable	Stable
Considerate	Lively	Supportive
Cooperative	Logical	Tactful
Dedicated	Loyal	Thoughtful
Democratic	Mathematical	Trustworthy
Discreet	Mature	Truthful
Eager	Merry	Understanding
Earnest	Motivating	Unique
Empathetic	Mysterious	Vigilant
Energetic	Natural	Vital
Enthusiastic	Nice	Warm
Fair	Noble	Well-Balanced
Flexible	Objective	Wholesome
Friendly	Organized	Wise
Forgiving	Open	Witty
Generous		

I Am Unique!

1. Write your name on the head of the outlined figure below and choose words from the word list to describe yourself.

2. Cut "yourself" out and mount yourself on a sheet of construction paper.

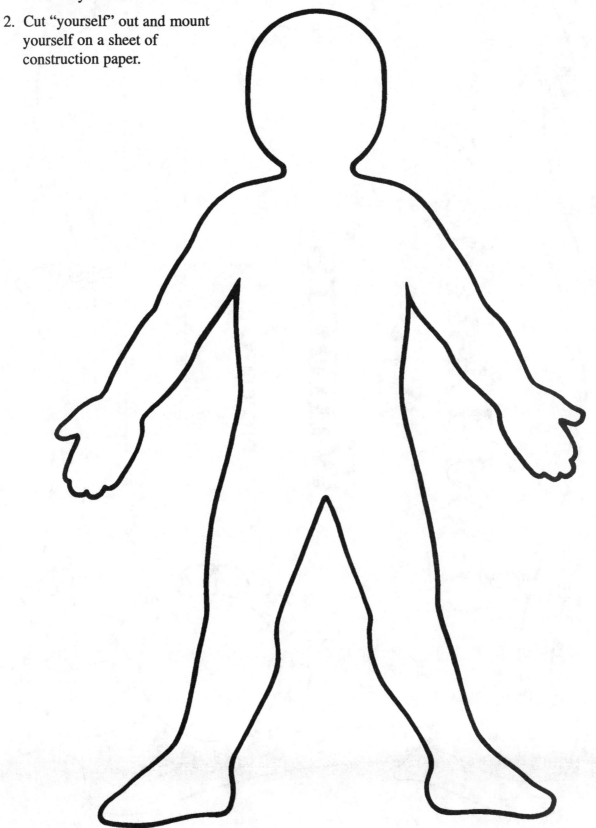

Good Listeners Are Winners!

presented to

_____

Date _____

_____

Signed _____

Using Your Senses

Objective

to enable the student to become aware of how important listening skills are and how to improve listening skills

Activity

1. Pre-record or bring to class a recorded passage from a book or some poems. Choose something that is unfamiliar to your students. The piece should be about 10–15 minutes long. This ensures that concentration is needed on the part of the student.

Suggested Passages:

Gibran, Kahlil. *The Prophet*. Alfred A. Knopf, Inc., 1923. (any of the selections, especially on "Friendship," "Self-Knowledge," and "Freedom")

Main, C. F. and Peter J. Seng. *Poems*. Wadsworth Publishing Company, Inc., 1961.

"Richard Cory" by Edwin Arlington Robinson—page 4

"Song" by John Donne—page 214

"Get Up and Bar the Door," Anonymous—page 68

(Note: This is a handbook and an anthology that gives teaching suggestions for the poems as well as the complete verse. It is an excellent addition to your bookshelf.)

2. Play the recording and ask your students to listen to the passage.

3. Then elicit from the students what the recording is about. Ask for details. Ask for the retelling of the story.

4. Survey how many of the students could accurately remember the details.

5. Pass out the How Well Do You Listen? activity sheet (page 100).

This lesson may be included in a science lesson about the ear.

Closure

Review the rules of good listening and speaking with your students.

How Well Do You Listen?

Think of all the senses you have. Think of the sense you used first. From the moment you were born, you used listening to perceive the world around you. Probably the first words you heard were those of your mother speaking softly in your ear.

Think of how you learned your language. It certainly was not from reading a book! It was through your sense of hearing. Did you imitate the sounds of your parents when learning to speak? Did you decode strange symbols in books in order to learn the meanings of the printed word? Did you try to recreate these symbols to write stories of your own? Of course you did!

Much of one's life depends on listening, so it is important to learn that with practice and perseverance one can become an excellent listener.

Answer the following questions:

1. What steps do you think you took to acquire English?

   _____

   _____

   _____

   _____

2. Do you listen as intently to the words you hear in school as you do to words heard on TV? To conversations at home?

   _____

   _____

3. Do you listen with the aim of repeating what you hear?

   _____

   _____

4. Do you ignore distractions in the classroom or outside?

   _____

   _____

5. Do you use your full concentration when someone is talking?

   _____

   _____

How to Be a Good Listener

Objective

to discuss with the students how listening affects school climate and behavior

Activity

1. Write the following words and phrases on the board. This may be done all at once or one at a time.

> ABCDEFGHIJKLMNOPQRSTUVWXYZ
>
> Listening to directions
>
> Listening with eyes
>
> Hearing
>
> Watching body language
>
> Actively listening
>
> Following instructions
>
> Tone of voice

2. Ask the students the following questions:
   - How does each word or phrase affect what you hear?
   - How is our school a better place when we have good listeners?
   - How would our classroom be a better place if we had good listeners?
   - Whom do you need to listen to at school? At home? On the campus? Other places you may go?
   - Is it important to be a good listener on a committee or a team?
   - Can you get your job done at school if you do not listen?
   - How do you feel when others are not listening to you?
   - Do you let others finish speaking before you start telling something?
   - Do adults, teachers included, need to listen? Why?

After you have had a group discussion with your class, have them create "Good Listener" posters. These then can be displayed around the class as a reminder for the students.

Instructions to Students

Today we are going to create "Good Listener" posters. Use the following page as a design plan for your work. Keep in mind all the things we discussed about listening. Now think of your own Good Listening reminders and create your poster. Make your posters colorful and eye catching and most of all make sure they remind people of how they need to listen.

I Hear You!

(Good Listener Poster Plan)

How Do You Learn?

Objective

A current trend in education appears to be the concept of multiple intelligences. It is the belief that people acquire knowledge in different ways, and some of these particular ways of learning are stronger than others. This theory of multiple intelligences was developed by Howard Gardner, a cognitive psychologist Many books and manuals that detail his theory can be found in public and college libraries, as well as local bookstores. The bibliography in this book contains a few.

To simplify Gardner's theory for our purposes, he believes that knowledge is acquired by individuals in seven different ways that he refers to as *intelligences*. These intelligences are characterized by a distinctive set of operations and developmental history. Although one or more may be stronger in any individual, they all are used in acquiring knowledge.

Gardner further states that if teachers or students were familiar with these seven intelligences and were aware of how they learn, the manner in which instruction is offered could be modified to meet the needs of the students.

Howard Gardner's Seven Styles of Learning

People learn in different ways. In fact there are several ways in which your students acquire knowledge. Of these, seven appear to be the most agreed upon by educators. They are *linguistic, logical, spatial, musical, kinesthetic, interpersonal,* and *intrapersonal*. Knowing which ways your students learn best allows you to provide curriculum to meet their needs. It also enables the students to become more aware of what things they need to do to become more successful in school.

Activities

The following student pages will provide your students with material on how the brain works, the seven different learning styles, and how they as students learn best.

Brain Facts (page 104) can be reproduced as a hand-out for your students. It is a statement of facts about our brains.

The Brain (page 105) is a drawing of the brain and its parts. The functions of the parts are labeled. Again this can be reproduced for the students.

Right Brain-Left Brain (pages 106–108) is a self-assessment for your students to take that will determine if the student is predominantly right or left brained. Note: Students should be reminded that a person uses both sides of the brain equally to perform many activities, and they should not think one side of the brain shuts down when the other side is working.

The Seven Styles of Learning (page 109) is an overview of the seven multiple intelligences and their characteristics. Through a series of questions the students determine what style of learner they might be. Included in this activity are suggestions for the students to use to increase their learning modalities.

Brain Facts

1. Even though most people would describe the brain as a computer, there is not a computer that has been created that displays a mixture of emotions, delights in its own abilities, or can fall in love.

2. Brains have been around for millions of years, but computers have not. Man created computers to make their lives easier.

3. The human brain can be divided into three regions—the forebrain, the midbrain, and the hindbrain.. Each of these sections is responsible for a different function in the body, yet each works closely with the others.

4. All the sections of the brain do not have equal importance. The brain stem, for example, has more importance because it regulates heart rate, breathing, and blood pressure, which are vital to the body's survival.

5. About one hundred million cells make up the central nervous system. Most of these are located in the brain's two hemispheres.

6. All one's mental processes, consciousness, learning, speech, thought, and recall are located in the part of the brain called the cerebrum.

7. The cerebrum has two parts—the left and the right hemispheres. The left hemisphere is the logical side of one's brain. The right hemisphere is the artistic side of one's brain.

8. Processes such as language, math skills, numeracy, and logic occur in the left brain.

9. Just as important, the right brain processes non-verbal, visio-spatial situations, and strategies of thinking.

10. Visual memory and musical talent are right brain functions. So are the ways in which we see the world: color, shape, and recognizing places.

The Brain

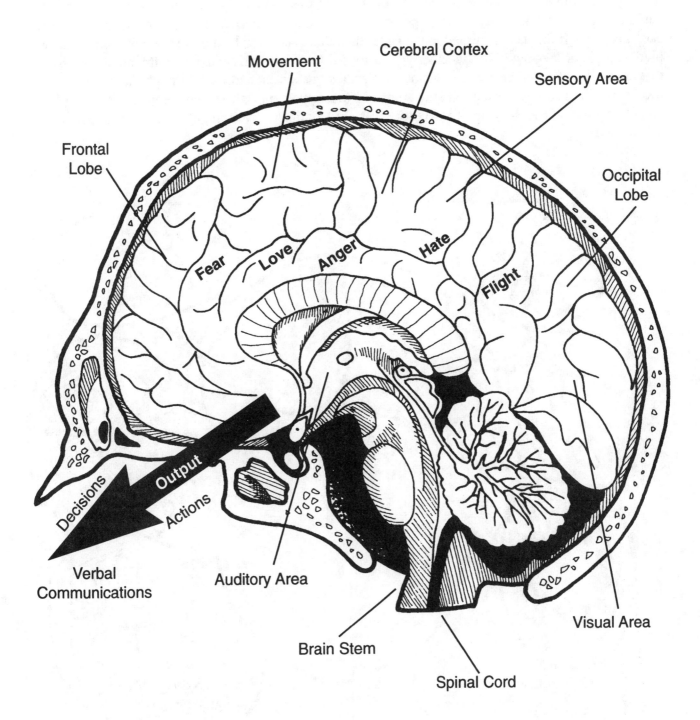

Movement

Cerebral Cortex

Sensory Area

Frontal Lobe

Occipital Lobe

Fear Love Anger Hate Flight

Decisions Output Actions

Verbal Communications

Auditory Area

Visual Area

Brain Stem

Spinal Cord

Right Brain/Left Brain

Now that you know a little about the brain, let's find out if you are right- or left-brained. Some scientists believe that the preference one shows by turning one's head is related to one's choice of work. For example, if the head is turned to the left, there is a tendency for that person to prefer non-verbal, right-brained activities. Such a person might be interested in the fields of music or the arts as a career choice. If the head is turned to the right, then there seems to be a preference for activities that involve logic or language. But whether you turn your head left or right is not as important as knowing that both sides of your brain work together and send signals back and forth through the nerves. Moreover, that is not really a good indication of whether you are right- or left-brained; however, by completing the Self-Assessment for Right/Left Brain Dominance, you might have a better idea of your dominance.

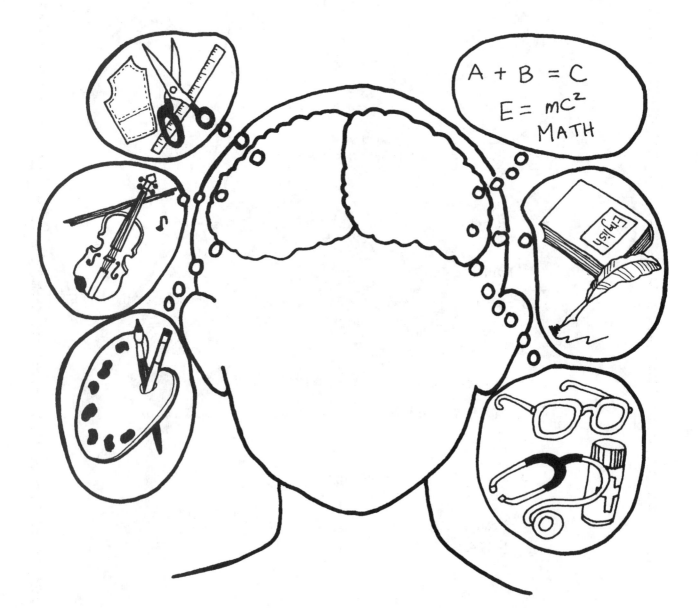

Self-Assessment for Right/Left Brain Dominance

Be truthful in answering these questions. Put a check mark next to the ones you feel are most appropriate.

☐ 1. I would rather take a true/false test, multiple choice test, or a matching test than an essay test.

☐ 2. I seem to learn best if I can see a process demonstrated or I can read the directions.

☐ 3. I dislike taking risks, and I like to be in control of a situation.

☐ 4. I think of many things at once instead of thinking through one thought at a time.

☐ 5. When I have a problem to solve, I try to divide it into smaller parts and solve it piece by piece.

☐ 6. I see problems or pictures as a whole rather than in parts or in details.

☐ 7. I have little or no difficulty in deciding what is right and what is wrong.

☐ 8. When I meet a person for the first time, I always remember that person's face, but I usually forget the name.

☐ 9. I solve most problem activities logically and analytically.

☐ 10. I usually use my imagination and think in abstracts.

☐ 11. I usually do not lose track of the time.

☐ 12. I tend to look for similarities rather than differences in things.

☐ 13. I read and follow written directions carefully and prefer to write my thoughts rather than speak.

☐ 14. I can usually remember things by recalling where I saw them on the page.

Self-Assessment for Right/Left Brain Dominance *(cont.)*

❏ 15. I can write instructions in a clear and logical manner.

❏ 16. I do well in geometry and geography.

❏ 17. I learn vocabulary easily.

❏ 18. When working in a group, I can usually sense the mood of others.

❏ 19. I prefer to plan ahead and be aware of what is going on.

❏ 20. I am emotional and often let my feelings out.

❏ 21. I sometimes whisper to myself to help me understand or remember a topic.

❏ 22. I am somewhat spontaneous.

❏ 23. I remember both jokes and punch lines.

❏ 24. I am usually aware of what everyone else is doing in class.

❏ 25. I can really concentrate when I desire.

❏ 26. People think I am creative, and they have told me so.

❏ 27. Mathematical concepts are easily understandable.

❏ 28. I can always remember melodies and tunes that I have heard.

❏ 29. I like to be orderly in most things.

❏ 30. I learn best by touching or doing.

Tally the total odd questions you checked and the total even numbers you checked; then put your answers below.

Number of odd questions _____ = left-brain activity.

Number of even questions _____ = right-brain activity.

Seven Styles of Learning

Objective

to make students aware of their learning styles

Activity

1. Distribute the Seven Intelligences Questionnaire (page 110) to your students.

2. Have them complete the questionnaire as carefully and honestly as possible.

3. After the questionnaire has been completed, distribute the Seven Types of Intelligence sheets (pages 111–112).

4. Instruct the students to compare their responses to the types of learners they might be.

5. After each student has had time to compare responses for each style of learning, discuss each of the styles. Allow sufficient time for a thorough discussion. Too little time might result in the students becoming confused.

Included below this activity is a "Teacher Reference" list suggesting some of the many ways in which you can provide for each of the seven intelligences.

The Seven Multiple Intelligences

Logical/Mathematical Intelligence

Often called "scientific thinking," this intelligence deals with numbers, recognizing abstract patterns, and inductive and deductive thinking and reasoning.

Visual/Spatial Intelligence

This intelligence relies on the sense of sight and being able to visualize an object. This person has the ability to create internal mental images and pictures.

Body/Kinesthetic Intelligence

This is the intelligence of physical movement and the wisdom of the body's movement. This knowledge involves the brain's motor cortex, which controls bodily motion.

Musical/Rhythmic Intelligence

This intelligence is based on the recognition of tonal patterns, including various environmental sounds, and on a sensitivity to rhythm and beats.

Interpersonal Intelligence

This intelligence operates primarily through person-to-person relationships and communication.

Intrapersonal Intelligence

This intelligence relates to inner states of being—self-reflection, metacognition (thinking about thinking), and awareness of spiritual realities.

Verbal/Linguistic Intelligence

This intelligence, which is related to words and language (both written and spoken), dominates most Western educational systems.

Seven Intelligences Questionnaire

Answer each question carefully and honestly.

1. What activities might you do in your free time?_____

2. What is your favorite subject in school?_____

3. What subject is the easiest? _____ The hardest? _____

4. Do you ever write stories or poems just for fun? _____

5. Do you prefer to go to a movie or go to a dance? _____

6. Do you enjoy working with other people? _____

7. Do you prefer to be by yourself?_____

8. Do you play an instrument? _____

9. Do you daydream?_____

10. Are you good at puzzles and mazes?_____

11. Do you enjoy having your own space? _____

12. Do you like to hum melodies and tunes? _____

13. Do you find yourself tapping tunes with your fingers? _____

14. Do you join clubs or groups of people? _____

15. Are you good at sports?_____

16. Do you use your hands when you talk? _____

17. Do you enjoy figuring things out? _____

18. Do you like doing experiments? _____

19. Do you like to tell stories? _____

20. Do you wear the same type of clothes others wear, or do you prefer your own style? _____

_____

Now compare you responses to the *Seven Styles of Learning* sheet to see what type of learner you are. Some people use more than one style when they learn. That is just fine, but try to pick the one that closely resembles the learning style you seem to favor most.

Seven Types of Intelligence

Find your dominant types of intelligence on the chart below. Then read and notice all the activities that would interest you. Try some new ones.

The Verbal/Linguistic Learner likes to . . .

- read

- write stories

- tell stories

- memorize things

- be humorous

- speak in public

The Logical/Mathematical Learner likes . . .

- abstract symbols

- outlining

- number sequences

- calculations

- problem solving

- pattern games

The Body/Kinesthetic Learner likes to . . .

- dance

- role play

- act in drama

- exercise physically

- mime

- invent things

- participate in sports

Seven Types of Intelligence *(cont.)*

The Musical/Rhythmic Learner likes to . . .

- write music

- hum

- sing

- dance

- play instruments

- attend musical performances

The Visual/Spatial Learner likes . . .

- color schemes

- patterns and designs

- drawing

- sculpting

- using an active imagination

The Interpersonal Learner likes . . .

- cooperative learning

- person-to-person communication

- group projects

- being empathetic

- receiving feedback

The Intrapersonal Learner likes . . .

- reflecting on things

- focus and concentration skills

- thinking strategies

- introspective practices

Goal-Setting Activity

Now that you have learned how you learn best and what type of learner you are, create a list of goals for the third quarter to better yourself.

At the end of the quarter reflect on your accomplishments and your failures if any.

Goals for the Third Quarter

_____

_____

_____

_____

_____

_____

_____

_____

_____

_____

Reflections:

_____

_____

Successes	Failures
_____	_____
_____	_____
_____	_____
_____	_____

Third Quarter

Life Skills

- Peer and Family Relationships
- Peer Pressure
- Drugs
- Gangs
- Conflict Resolution
- Prejudice
- Cultural Awareness

Study Skills/Research
Goal Setting

I Am What I Am

Objective

to help students be aware of and understand how members of the opposite sex view them and their behavior

Activity

1. Separate the boys from the girls.

2. Instruct each of the groups to write down a description of the opposite sex in their age level. Ask each group to choose a representative to speak for them. Allow 5–15 minutes for this.

3. When time is up, call the groups together.

4. Let each representative express the group's ideas. Allow approximately five minutes.

5. Allow approximately five minutes for the other group to present a rebuttal.

6. When both groups have had a chance to express all their opinions, elicit whether their views of the opposite sex have changed and how or why.

Helpful Hints for Each Group

1. Include a description of how the other group behaves in general. Cite a few examples and write down several things you think are important.

2. What do you think of that behavior?

3. How would you like them to act?

4. What behaviors are becoming to the group?

5. What behaviors are unbecoming to the group?

Closure

After the presentation, ask the groups to separate once again and have them each compile a list of the things they learned about the other group's behaviors.

A follow-up session may be one in which these lists are reviewed and opinions aired.

Mistakes in Relating

Objective

to make students aware of the social mistakes that they might make in a social situation

Activity

1. Set the stage for discussion by asking the students if they have ever made a quick judgment about another person without having enough information.

2. Ascertain from the students what mistakes they have made. Write a list of these mistakes on the board.

3. Divide your class into groups of four to five and have them discuss the following:

   - Which mistakes do you make most often?

   - In what type of environment do you tend to make these mistakes?

   - Is there any way that these mistakes can be avoided?

   - What advice can you give a person who repeatedly makes mistakes?

   - What changes should this person make?

4. Allow 15–20 minutes for the groups to discuss the problems and then call the group together.

5. Have each group report what was discussed and what solutions they arrived at.

6. Then conclude this activity with a round-robin discussion of the following:

   - Making a quick decision about another without enough information

   - Letting the first impression affect a relationship

   - Expecting others to be the way you think they should be

   - Looking for weaknesses in others instead of strengths

   - Failing to understand that how another person views himself/herself affects his/her behavior.

Conclusion

Using a long piece of butcher paper, place the following as the heading: *Mistakes in Relating.* Hang the butcher paper along the classroom hall. Have your students complete the exercise on page 117 and post it on the butcher paper to display for a week or two so that they may reflect on what they discussed.

Mistakes in Relating *(cont.)*

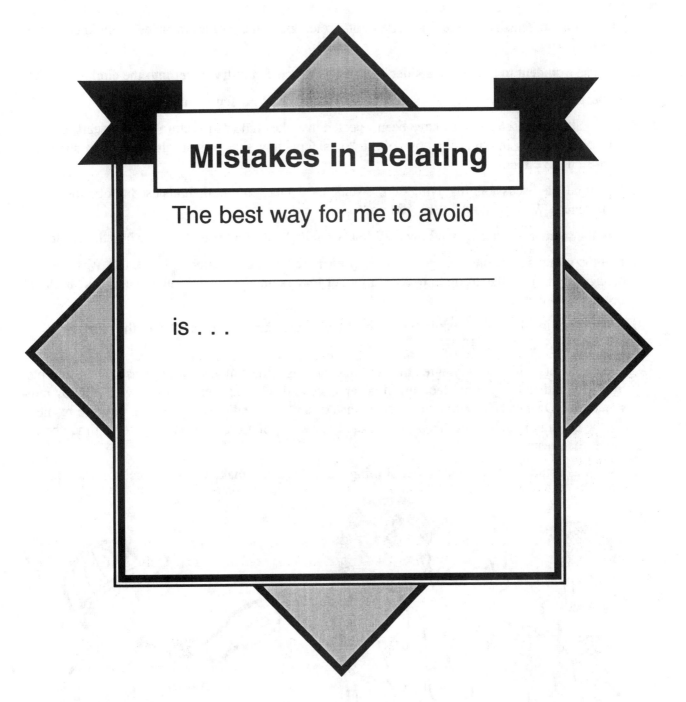

Mistakes in Relating

The best way for me to avoid

_____

is . . .

May I Join Your Group?

Objective

to allow students to become aware of how it feels when members of a group reject them

Activity

1. Have your students sit on the floor in a tight circle. Have them cross their legs with knees touching.

2. Choose a student to be "The Outsider." Instruct that person to try to get into the circle.

3. Repeat this process with various students. Do not have any discussion at this time.

4. When all the chosen students have been rejected, ask the students to return to their seats and initiate the discussion by asking one of the "outsiders" how that person felt when he or she tried to breach the circle.

5. Continue the discussion, involving all the students. Question the methods used to obtain admittance. What worked? What did not?

6. Ask the members of the group how they felt when an "outsider" tried to break into the circle.

7. Did the group's reactions change in any way as more "outsiders" tried to break in? Was the change (if any) for the group to become more or less exclusive as additional "outsiders" tried to become members?

8. What behaviors have they exhibited when a new student arrives in class? Are they Freddy Friendly or Sally Standoffish?

9. Most students will probably agree that an "outsider" is almost always very pleased to be accepted by a group, thereby gaining feelings of acceptance and self-confidence—positive results by most standards. Does the class think that acceptance of an "outsider" has any similar positive results for the existing members of the group? Exactly how might a group benefit by adding members rather than restricting them?

10. Lastly, ask students to compile a list of things they can do to make outsiders feel comfortable.

If You Can't Say Anything Nice . . .

Objective

to promote skill in a habit that all of us, teachers included, could use more practice in—that is, COMPLIMENTS!

Activity

1. Write the words "Mutual Understanding" on the board.

2. Ask for the definition of those words. Basically this means that when people interact, they do so in ways that will benefit both of them.

3. Mutual understanding is important to most pre-teens and teens.

4. Explain to the students that all of us want to be perceived and recognized for the qualities we possess.

5. Then explain that today we are going to learn how to give and receive compliments—without embarrassment!

6. Distribute white construction paper to the students. 8 ½" x 11" (21.5 cm x 27.5 cm) is perfect.

7. Fold your paper into eighths. Ask the students to make personal statements on each card for their fellow classmates. Write the classmate's name on the front of the card and the sender's name on the back.

8. Tell the students to look for individual accomplishments such as personal grooming, good grades, hobbies, talents, and special feats of endeavor.

9. Teachers, do not forget to make your own compliment cards for your students.

10. When a classmate gives you a compliment, say "Thank You" and smile.

Closure

Many students become so involved in this activity that they want to continue doing it. Some extensions are the following:

- Make your own calling card. Create a logo that reflects you.

- On poster board, mount the compliments you have received and write an autobiographical sketch about yourself.

- Draw a self-portrait of your head and put all the complimentary words in your head. Put a huge smile on your face.

Self-Portrait

Draw a picture of yourself when you are at your happiest.	Draw a picture of yourself when you are at your saddest.

Draw a picture of yourself as you think others see you.

If Johnny Jumps off a Bridge, Will You Follow?

Objective

to help students realize that they are individuals and that no two people are exactly alike—not even twins

Activity

1. Ask your students if they have ever heard anything like the question asked in the page title above. It is safe to say that most of them probably have by now. It usually is the answer to that classic complaint, "But Mom, everybody else is going!"

2. Ask your students why they think this kind of phrase was used? Most will say it was because "my parents did not want me to do something."

3. Explain that this might be true, but what is also true is that each of us is unique and different, that there are no two people who are exactly alike—not even twins. If you have twins in your class, have them explain how they differ from each other.

4. Have all students write down the qualities which they think make them unique. Then have them choose a classmate and write down that person's special qualities. There are to be no negatives—only positives.

5. Allow time for completion and have a short discussion about what the students wrote and why.

6. Distribute white paper to the students on which to mount their special positive qualities as seen by their classmates. This will become their own graffiti board in the classroom on which to display unique qualities about themselves.

7. Those students who would like to display their graffiti should be allowed to, although no one should be forced to.

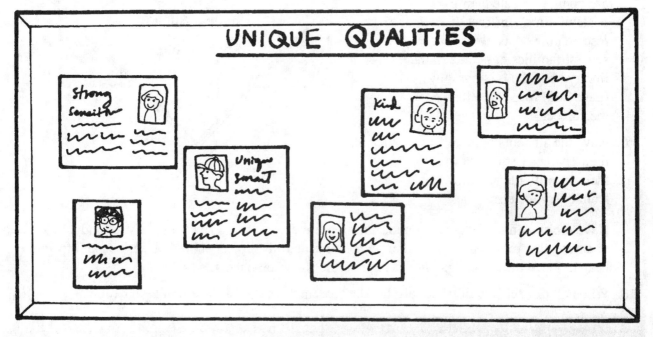

A Coat of Arms

Objective

to provide the students with the opportunity to view personal preferences as they relate to their self-awareness

Activity

1. Say, "Today we are going to make our own personal coats of arms." Then show the picture on the following page and tell the students that this is your coat of arms. Middle schoolers love this type of humor.

2. After the giggles and laughs, ask if anyone knows what a coat of arms is, why they were used, and when.

3. If the students cannot answer, use the time for research.

4. When the answers are found, discuss the information and what was unique about each family's coat of arms.

   Some answers might be . . .

   • the coat of arms reflects where the person lives.

   • the coat of arms tells something important about a person.

   • the coat of arms shows the strengths of a person to the world.

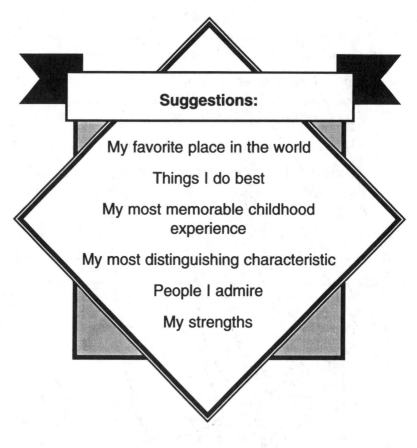

Suggestions:

My favorite place in the world

Things I do best

My most memorable childhood experience

My most distinguishing characteristic

People I admire

My strengths

5. Explain to the students that they are going to create their own coats of arms. Instruct them to research the coats of arms of several families or people in the library. See the bibliography (page 265) for suggestions on the subject.

6. Have the students write a list of their characteristics that make them identifiable and different from everyone else.

7. Have the students now draw symbols that represent some of these characteristics and add a motto or saying that represents one of their highest ideals (this project should be serious and from the heart). Place these elements in a design on the shield on page 124.

8. When all projects are finished, display the students' coats of arms around your room.

A Coat of Arms *(cont.)*

My Coat of Arms

Use the shield below or research the coat of arms in history and design your own.

124

Peer Pressure

When students understand themselves and have a strong, positive self-image, they are less likely to become involved with gangs or drugs. In addition to this, students also need to realize the types of relationships they have with the people they will meet throughout their lives. It is important for them to understand that relationships go through stages, and sometimes people who are our friends today might not be our friends tomorrow.

Students are being exposed to more information today than ever before. Mass communication has enabled them to see more of the world than ever before. Unfortunately mass communication has also presented students with some of the seediest environments in our world, which they may perceive in a mistaken manner.

Drug dealers and gang leaders are sometimes portrayed as having lots of money, control, and all the glitter that most students do not have at home. Some students may be led to feel that these visions are so glamorous that they represent just what those students want from life.

Peer pressure, of course, exists at all levels of growth following infancy, but it begins to reach powerful amplification during the middle school years. The young adolescent begins to experience intense periods of self-consciousness and growing desires for group acceptance and approval which may in some cases override parental or other adult influence, much to the dismay of parents and teachers. Perhaps more than at any other time, students during these vulnerable years need strong leadership and guidance to help them cope with distracting and destructive influences of our turbulent society.

The following activities will help your students' understanding of the following serious matters:

- Relationships
- Gangs and Gang Violence
- Conflict and Conflict Resolution

Relationships

Relationships are based upon common interests and goals. When we meet someone for the first time, we try to look for those things we might have in common and base the relationship on that. For example, let's say you like to play tennis, and so does your new classmate. The first conversations or outings might revolve around the game of tennis. If you find that you have much in common with a person, that person might eventually become your friend. Not everyone you meet throughout your life, of course, will become your friend. Some will always remain acquaintances. In either case, different people bring new thoughts and opinions to your world.

Understanding yourself and others will help you in your relationships with other people.

Most relationships go through the following stages:

1. **Initiating**

   This is the first contact you have with someone new. You find that you are interested in making conversation, and conversation might be nothing more than a few words.

2. **Experimenting**

   During the experimental stage you find out what interests you might have in common. You might first ask where that person went to school or where that person lived before coming to your school. Some people sometimes call this stage "small talk."

3. **Intensifying**

   This stage is where the relationship becomes stronger. You find yourself doing lots of things together, and you might find yourself talking to this person much of the time.

4. **Integrating**

   During integration your relationship strengthens. There is a strong commitment to our friends. Loyalty is fierce, and many people would do almost anything for their friends.

5. **Bonding**

   Bonding occurs when friends want to do the same things together. If you are invited to a party and your friend is not, then you might ask the party giver to include your friend or you might decide not to go yourself. Many of the activities that you do, you do with your friend. This is the stage most commonly referred to as "best friends."

6. **Differentiating**

   Togetherness is not always wonderful. Sometimes we feel the need to be our own person and want to do some activities on our own or with others. We seek to be unique and individual. Sometimes this can be a turning point in relationships. One person may resent the fact that you do not want to do everything with him or her. Feelings can be hurt, and the relationship can grow apart. On the other hand, your friends may understand and want the same uniqueness for themselves, and so differentiating can be both a positive and a negative stage.

Relationships *(cont.)*

7. Circumscribing

So far, all the stages have referred to the growth of friendships. Circumscribing is the first stage in the decline of the relationship. At this stage you might decide to go to the game with other friends, or go to that party your friend was not invited to. This does not mean that you never want to be friends. It just means that you want your own space and need other people in your life.

8. Stagnation

If circumscribing continues, the relationship begins to stagnate. Stagnation is defined as a period of no growth. Things remain the same. You may not call your friend as often, if at all. You find you have nothing to say. You may still go to a movie, but things are just not the same anymore, and you find that you have much more fun with other people.

9. Avoiding

This is when you would rather not have anything to do with that person anymore. You might take a different street home from school just to avoid seeing that person. You might have your mom tell that person that you are not home when he or she calls.

10. Termination

This is the end—the final stage in a relationship. Both of you go your own ways with different groups of people. You do not see or talk to each other except for the cordial "Hi" around school.

Clearly, all relationships do not follow rigidly the pattern of growth and decline outlined above. Some relationships simply do not develop enough for one to experience all stages. Still others reach a mature stage of bonding and never really decline. Lifetime friendships are made of such stuff. Nevertheless, these are classic pictures of the different stages of development in the vast majority of relationships experienced by most people.

Experimenting *Integrating* *Differentiating*

Evaluating Your Relationships

Think of a time in the recent past when you might have met someone new. What type of relationship did you have with this person?

Do you find it easy or difficult to make new acquaintances? Explain your answer.

Take a close look at the relationships you have with your peers. On the lines below choose five of those people and decide which stage of relationship you have with them.

Name	Type of Relationship
1.	
2.	
3.	
4.	
5.	

Look for cartoons in the newspaper or in magazines that reflect the stages in relationships and create a poster for display.

Friendship

Objective

to enable students to understand the relationship between an acquaintance and a friend

Activity

1. Elicit from your students their definitions of *friend*. Write them on the board.

2. Ask "What is necessary for friendship?" Write their answers on the board.

3. Read the selection on What Makes a Friend (page 130) and see if it corresponds with what is written on the board.

4. Distribute the Friendship Activity sheet (page 131) to your students.

5. Have the students search magazines and newspapers for examples of friendships. Cut the samples out and put them in a pile.

Then have the students choose a picture. Supply them with the picture frame (page 132) and have them paste the picture into the frame. They are to write a history about the people in the picture. Who are they and what might they be thinking or doing? How do you think they became friends?

What Makes a Friend?

Friendship is a special kind of relationship. Some friendships are so strong that they can last for a lifetime and over many miles of separation. Maybe you have a friend who lives in another city, state, or even another country that you still keep close contact with.

Think for a moment what it takes to keep that friendship going. Do you write letters or visit each other when possible? Do you confide your innermost feelings to that friend?

Well, you probably have a variety of friends and even a few who can be considered special friends. In 1984, an article published in the *Journal of Social and Personal Relationships* (1984): 211–37 titled "The Rules of Friendship," Michael Argyle and Monika Henderson found six rules that distinguish friends from other relationships.

These six rules are very important for the friendship to grow and survive. They are listed below:

1. Stand up for one another when you are apart.

2. Share the news of success with the other person.

3. Show emotional support.

4. Trust and confide in each other.

5. Volunteer to help in a time of need.

6. Strive to make the other happy when you are together.

Friendship Activity

Read the six Rules of Friendship again.

Think of some of the friends you have and your relationships with them. Does your friendship meet all the rules? Explain why or why not on the lines below.

_____

_____

_____

_____

_____

_____

_____

_____

_____

_____

Many times friendships just wither away. As sad as this change may be, there are many reasons for this to happen. Some of these reasons we can control, and some we cannot. Think of some of the many reasons a friendship might wither and die. Write them on the lines below.

_____

_____

_____

_____

_____

_____

_____

A Picture Is Worth a Thousand Words

Choose the picture of your choice from those supplied. Glue the picture inside the frame and write about the events that led to the moment the picture was taken. Tell about the people in the picture and create a friendship for them.

A Collage of Famous Friends

A collage is a collection of pictures arranged in a pleasing manner that revolves around a special theme.

The theme of your collage is *Friendship.*

Look through magazines, newspapers, and comic books and find some famous friendships. Cut out the pictures and create a collage of famous friends. To help you get started, Batman and Robin are famous friends. So were The Lone Ranger and Tonto. It is easy to find many more.

After creating your collage, write about one famous pair you chose. Be sure to detail what made these fictitious pairs such good friends, or (if you do not know) you may make up a story that explains how the original friendship started. You must make the story consistent with the characters, of course. (You would not want Tonto to first meet the Lone Ranger when they were very young and battling crime on the streets of Gotham City, for example. Silver and Scout would not be able to maneuver through the traffic very well.)

The Friendship Award

presented to

_____

_____
Date

_____
Signed

Decisions, Decisions

Objective

to develop some decision-making tools that will assist middle school students in making the right choices

Activity

1. For three or four days have your students bring in the newspaper or news magazines.

2. When there is sufficient material for all students, have them look through the newspapers and magazines to find some articles about people facing problems.

3. Have the students choose one of the articles and have them write what the problem is and how the person involved might go about solving it.

4. Then have the students pretend that they are "Dear Abby" and have them write what advice they would give those people in trouble.

5. Give each student a chance to tell about the news story and the advice he or she would give these people.

6. Using the suggestions of the students, compile a list of those decision-making skills that the students feel would be useful to them.

7. Have the students write those skills on the Decisions, Decisions activity sheets (pages 136–137) and place them in their binders for reference when they might need them.

8. Continue this activity by asking the students to list 10 things that they are not allowed to do.

9. Have them choose the three things that they feel are the most restrictive, and ask them to star or highlight these on their Decision, Decisions sheet.

10. Have the students complete the page.

11. Break into small groups and have the students discuss the similarities and differences in their problems. It may surprise them to find that they have similar problems and restrictions.

Decisions, Decisions *(cont.)*

1. List the decision-making skills the class used in solving the problems presented in the newspaper and magazine articles.

_____

_____

_____

_____

_____

_____

_____

_____

_____

_____

2. Write 10 things that you are not allowed to do.

a. _____

b. _____

c. _____

d. _____

e. _____

f. _____

g. _____

h. _____

i. _____

j. _____

Decisions, Decisions *(cont.)*

3. Answer the following about your restrictions:

   a. What problems might arise if you were allowed to do the above activities?

   _____

   _____

   _____

   b. Do restrictions tend to create or resolve problems? _____ Why or why not?

   _____

   _____

   _____

   c. *"C'est la Vie!"* (pronounced Say-la-Vee) is French for "That's life!" This is what French people say when something happens that they cannot control. No one can control everything in life. Write about a problem you had that you could not avoid.

   _____

   _____

   _____

   _____

   _____

   _____

4. Sometimes you make bad decisions. (Even adults make bad decisions from time to time.) If you do make a bad decision, do you have the option to change it? Why or why not?

   _____

   _____

   _____

   _____

   _____

   _____

   _____

   _____

Banishing Bad Habits

Objective

to allow the students to become aware of their bad habits and learn what they can do to overcome them

Materials

- lightweight poster board
- variety of markers, crayons, colored pencils
- decorations to add to the masks—feathers, sequins, fabric scraps, yarn, ribbon, yarn, 3-D O's purchased from a craft shop, etc.
- glue or a glue gun
- small wooden stick or dowel for each student (for mask mounting)

Procedure

1. Discuss bad habits—what they are and how we develop them.

2. Discuss the feelings and emotions generated when practicing bad habits.

3. Discuss how faces reveal different feelings and emotions. Students may take turns acting out different emotions, and the class may guess the emotions they are trying to portray.

   Following are some emotions that are perfect for acting out:

fear	confusion	disappointment
joy	surprise	jealousy
anger	excitement	sadness
pain	frustration	embarrassment
regret	shock	anxiety

4. Have each student design and create a mask which shows one emotion.

5. Collectively develop some words and phrases that express the various emotions discussed. Let each student select his or her own list of words for his or her mask.

6. Have each student write about a situation when he or she felt the emotion displayed in his or her mask.

7. When masks and writing are completed, display them in an attractive manner around the room.

8. If a video camera is available, film the students acting out their emotions. Play this video at open house in the spring.

Good Decisions for Bad Habits

Self-Study

Complete this self-study sheet. Be a deep thinker and be honest. If you cannot be honest with yourself, then this activity cannot help you to improve.

- Make a list of some of your bad habits.

_____

_____

_____

_____

_____

- What habits would you like to change?

_____

_____

_____

_____

_____

- How do you think you might change these habits?

_____

_____

_____

_____

_____

- Whose help, if any, would you need to change these habits?

_____

_____

_____

_____

_____

Good Decisions for Bad Habits *(cont.)*

Habits are sometimes hard to break. Sometimes tiny steps are needed before we can reach our goal. What tiny steps can you take to make a bad habit disappear?

- How long do you think it might take for you to change your habit?

  _____

  _____

- If you do not succeed in making a change, what can you do?

  _____

  _____

  _____

  _____

- Sometimes, even though we have good intentions, it is terribly hard to break a habit (like smoking for adults). If this should happen to you, what do you think would be the best way to proceed?

  _____

  _____

  _____

  _____

  _____

  _____

  _____

  _____

  _____

  _____

  _____

  _____

The Deep Thinker Award

presented to

_____

Date _____

Signed _____

Make the Right Choice

Objective

to help students learn that problems are a normal part of life and that by recognizing problems, students are better able to deal with them in a logical and constructive manner

Materials

- assorted empty medicine tubes, bottles, and jars (cleaned, washed, and dried before the students handle them)
- various empty prescription-labeled medicine containers supplied by the teacher
- various magazines that students are able to cut up

Activity

1. Display the various medicine containers on a desk before the class.

2. Ask the students to tell you what these items are and why they think you have brought them to class. Accept all reasonable answers.

3. Most students will respond that they are medicines and maybe someone is ill.

4. Choose a few of your students to come up before the class and separate the drugs from the medicines.

   (All drugs can be medicines, if a highly trained professional prescribes them for an individual's use and they are medically supervised.)

5. Begin the discussion by asking whether all medicines are drugs and whether there is a difference between a medicine and a drug.

6. When does a medicine become a drug?

7. What is a drug?

   (A drug is usually defined in most health books as tobacco, alcohol, all illegal substances, and any medicine which is being abused.)

8. Review with your students the harmful effects of drugs and the effects that drugs have on the body.

9. Have a student come up and separate the samples into the ones purchased over the counter and the ones prescribed by a doctor.

Make the Right Choice *(cont.)*

10. Elicit the differences between prescription and over-the-counter medicine. Some possible answers follow.

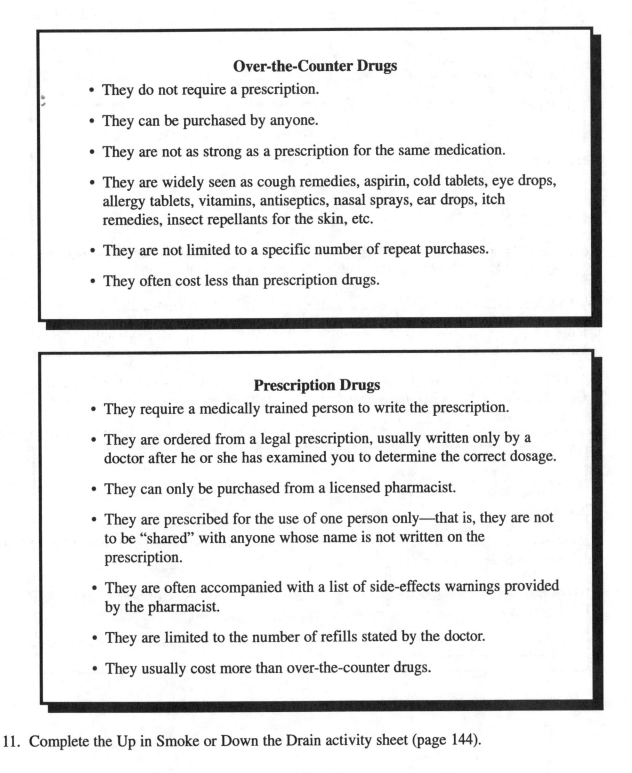

Over-the-Counter Drugs

- They do not require a prescription.

- They can be purchased by anyone.

- They are not as strong as a prescription for the same medication.

- They are widely seen as cough remedies, aspirin, cold tablets, eye drops, allergy tablets, vitamins, antiseptics, nasal sprays, ear drops, itch remedies, insect repellants for the skin, etc.

- They are not limited to a specific number of repeat purchases.

- They often cost less than prescription drugs.

Prescription Drugs

- They require a medically trained person to write the prescription.

- They are ordered from a legal prescription, usually written only by a doctor after he or she has examined you to determine the correct dosage.

- They can only be purchased from a licensed pharmacist.

- They are prescribed for the use of one person only—that is, they are not to be "shared" with anyone whose name is not written on the prescription.

- They are often accompanied with a list of side-effects warnings provided by the pharmacist.

- They are limited to the number of refills stated by the doctor.

- They usually cost more than over-the-counter drugs.

11. Complete the Up in Smoke or Down the Drain activity sheet (page 144).

Up in Smoke or Down the Drain

Calculate the cost of a person smoking a pack of cigarettes a day. You can find this out by asking someone who smokes or asking a store that carries cigarettes.

Assume a pack a day costs_____.

Calculate the cost of the following:

Cigarettes for a week _____ x 7 = _____

Cigarettes for a month _____ x 30 = _____

Cigarettes for a year _____ x 365 = _____

If a person is 65 years old and has smoked two packs of cigarettes a day since he was 15, how much money would he have spent on his bad habit?

_____

Calculate the cost of a person who drinks a six-pack of beer every day. Assume a six-pack costs_____ .

Beer for a week _____ x 7 = _____

Beer for a month _____ x 30 = _____

Beer for a year _____ x 365 = _____

If the person is now 72 years old and began drinking a six-pack of beer a day when he was 21, how much money would he have spent on his bad habit?

_____

What are some things that money (the total for beer and cigarettes) could purchase if it had not been used for drugs?

Research and Write

Objective

to allow the students to research a topic relating to the health and well-being of human beings

(Allow for a wide range of topics and keep your suggestions to a minimum. This allows the students a chance to make decisions for themselves. The suggested format for a research paper on the following pages may be utilized at your discretion.)

Activities

1. Explain to the students that they are going to write research papers on topics that relate to the various aspects of the human body.

2. Distribute the **Research Paper Format** sheets on pages 146–154.

3. Included for the students' instruction are these elements:

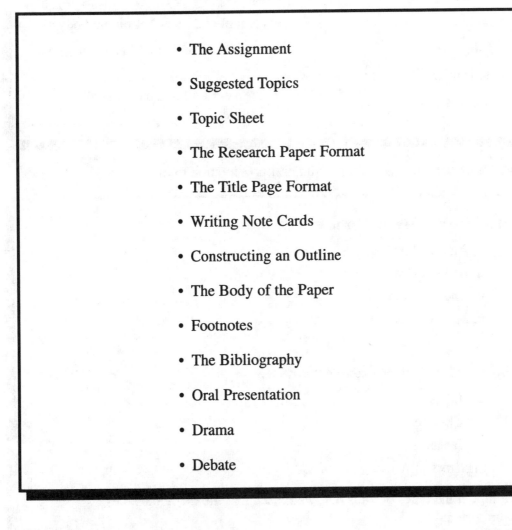

- The Assignment

- Suggested Topics

- Topic Sheet

- The Research Paper Format

- The Title Page Format

- Writing Note Cards

- Constructing an Outline

- The Body of the Paper

- Footnotes

- The Bibliography

- Oral Presentation

- Drama

- Debate

Note: The suggested forms are based on the MLA style of writing but may be modified to meet the method of writing your students are taught.

Human Body Research Paper

The Assignment

Your assignment is to write a research paper on a topic that relates to the human body. You may choose from any topic that interests you or from the suggestions below.

Your paper needs to be between 5–10 pages long and include pictures, drawings, graphs, or photographs that pertain to your topic. Your paper is required to have a title page and a bibliography. The following pages will give you guidelines to follow. Do not forget to use your English book, a dictionary, and a thesaurus if you need additional help.

Suggested Topics
- prescription drugs
- over-the-counter drugs
- antibiotics
- pain killers
- anti-inflammatory drugs
- steroids
- stimulants
- depressives
- alcohol and its effect on the body
- the history of Alcoholics Anonymous (AA)
- intervention for the chemically dependant

Choose one of the following topics and prepare an oral presentation to the class.

1. **Medicine and Medical Practices . . .**

   in Ancient Egypt
   in Ancient Greece
   in Ancient Rome
   in Medieval Europe
   in Ancient Asia

2. **Unusual Medical Practices Among . . .**

   the Indians
   the Chinese
   the Japanese
   the tribes in Africa

   (Find out the types of tools that were used and the medicines they administered.)

3. **Drugs and Their Effects on Unborn Babies**

4. **Drugs—Everybody's Problem**

Human Body Research Paper *(cont.)*

Once you have decided on your topic, write your choice below and have your parent or guardian sign the Topic Sheet and return it to your teacher.

(Cut here.)

The Topic Sheet

Dear Parent:

Your child has been assigned a human body research paper due on the following date:_____ Please supervise him/her in the completion of this assignment.

Thank you,

Student's Name: _____

Title of Research Paper: _____

Parent Signature:_____

Research Paper Format

The following are suggested guidelines for writing a research paper. Many teachers might have their own requirements too. So be sure to check with your teachers to see if they require something different.

Typing or Printing the Paper

Make sure your typewriter or printer has a fresh ribbon before you start to print your paper. Papers that are too light are difficult to read. Use only dark blue or black ink to write your paper. Use standard 8 ½" x 11" (21.25 cm x 27.5 cm) unlined white paper. The research paper is always double spaced and written on one side of the paper only. Do not draw, write, or mount anything on the other side of the paper. If you are going to handwrite your paper, write neatly and legibly, and do not erase unless it is absolutely necessary. Again, write on one side of the paper only.

Margins

Leave a one-inch (2.5 cm) margin around the top, bottom, and sides of the text. Indent five spaces for paragraphs and 10 spaces on both sides for quotes of three or more lines.

Heading and Title

Research papers do not need a title page unless required by your teacher. Simply type or write the title in capital letters. There is no need to underline the title.

Numbering the Pages

It is necessary for the pages of a research paper to be numbered in consecutive order in the upper right-hand corner of your page.

Folders or Covers

Bind your paper in a paper or plastic folder. Be sure your pages are secured tightly. Do not use other means of binding your papers. Although it may be more attractive to use other types of folders, they can be bulky and heavy.

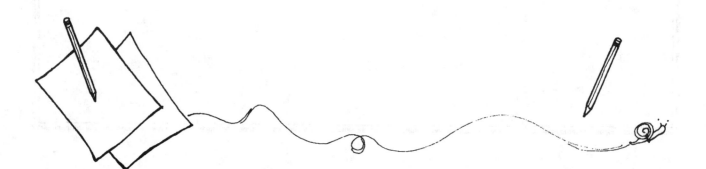

The Title Page

Use the following format for your paper

TITLE OF YOUR RESEARCH PAPER

By

Student's Name

Name of the Course, Period

Teacher's Name

Date

Note Cards

Note cards make information-gathering easy because they can be sorted, arranged, and rearranged. Note cards make writing your rough draft easier if you take the time to prepare them properly. They also save you the trouble of going back to the source for a missing name, title, or page number.

There are several different types of note cards. The type suggested below is a combination kind because it contains all the important information that you will use in your paper.

Use 3 ½" x 5" (8.75 cm x 12.5 cm) index cards.

A rubber band will keep your cards orderly and secure. The first card should contain the following information:

- Your Name
- Topic
- Date

The following cards are to be completed in the following manner.

- A source number should be written in the top right corner of the card. Numbers change when the author of your source changes.
- A key word should be written on the left side of the first line. This will help you locate similar topics when you begin your outline.
- The page number that you acquired the information from should be recorded.
- Any comments that you may want to make about your information should be put in parentheses.

Sample Card

```
                                                    1

  Children

  Heller, Sherri Z.  What Makes You So Special?
  Arizona.  1990.  Pages 26-30


  What are the things that children enjoy?
  (reading, game playing, and puzzles)
```

Model Entry

First Entry

> 1
>
> Author's last name, first name. Title of book.
>
> Place of publication. Year printed. Pages used.
>
> Information from source.
> (Your comments—optional.)

Other Cards from Same Source

> 1
>
> Author's last name.
>
> Page numbers.
>
> Information from source.
> (comments)

Notecard for a New Source

> 2
>
> Author's last name, first name. Title of source.
>
> Place of publication. Year printed. Pages used.
>
> Information from source.
> (comments)

The Outline

An outline is a simple summary which helps you organize and plan the paper you are going to write. The outline also helps you identify missing or irrelevant material and add material to those areas that are too short.

Follow the simple explanation below to complete your outline.

Main topics begin on the left margin, and items that are sub-concepts are indented. All main topics begin with Roman numerals; subconcepts follow with capital letters, then Arabic numbers, and finally lower case letters as the concepts become more specific. All lines of written work begin with a capital letter, and there are always at least two entries for each main topic or subconcept.

Sample Outline

Dogs

Dogs in today's society have two roles: as working dogs and as house pets.

I. Working Dogs

  A. Hunting

    1. Retrievers

      a. Golden

      b. Labrador

    2. Terriers

      a. Jack Russell—Eddie on "Frasier"

      b. Wire Haired

      c. Fox

  B. Tracking

    1. Hounds

      a. Blood Hounds

      b. Basset Hounds

    2. Doberman Pinschers

    3. St. Bernards

  C. Herding

    1. Collie

    2. Bearded Collie

    3. Sheepdog

  D. Guarding

    1. Rottweilers

    2. German Shepherds

    3. Doberman Pinchers

II. House Pets

  A. Small Breeds

    1. Shih Tzu

    2. Lhasa Apso

    3. Toy Poodle

  B. Medium Breeds

    1. Cocker Spaniel

    2. Scotch Terriers

  C. Large Breeds

    1. Airdales

    2. Alaskan Malamute

    3. Husky

Continue in this manner until you have outlined all the categories you have chosen.

The Body of the Research Paper

Introductory Paragraph

The introduction of your research paper is generally like an essay, only longer. The introduction contains a *thesis statement* or the statement of purpose. This statement should express what you are going to say in your paper.

The Body of the Paper

The body of the paper contains information on the various topics and sub-divisions with documented proof or evidence located by your research.

Conclusion

The conclusion is the summation of what you have said. It should restate the intent of your paper and the main points you wanted to make. It is your last summation of facts.

In moving from part to part, you should be certain to put in effective transitions (words or phrases that connect a previous topic with a new one) so the paper has good continuity. You should also give your paper an interesting title that will attract the reader's attention.

Hints to Make Your Paper Better

1. Limit the scope of your research. It would be impossible to write a paper on a topic like "Education" because the subject is too broad and there are too many sub-concepts.

2. Research papers are written in the third person. Avoid using "I" or giving your own opinion. Take the position of the newspaper reporter. In fact, you might want to read some newspaper articles to become familiar with the third person mode of expression.

3. Avoid very technical subjects, personal arguments, very recent subjects, and general biographies. Remember, this is a research paper. It should contain a factual reporting of information.

The Footnotes

Beginning in 1984, the recommendation of the Modern Language Association places citations (quotes) or sources directly in the text of the paper in parentheses. In this format, you list the sources in alphabetical order at the end of the essay in the bibliography.

How to Write a Quote

"Sweet Betsy From Pike," a folk song known to every California school child, survives from the period of the gold rush. This song has been reported as having the most variations in lyrics of all the songs connected with the gold rush (Dwyer and Lingenfelter, 42).

Notice that the punctuation for your sentence comes after the parenthetical note.

The Bibliography

The bibliography is an alphabetical listing of all the sources you used for your paper. Bibliographies are completed in a very specific manner, depending upon the type of source you use. The following is a listing of the more common source bibliographies. Ask your teacher to guide you if your source is different from the ones listed.

1. A book by a single author

   Clark, Kenneth. *What Is a Masterpiece?* London: Thames. 1979.

2. A book by two or more authors

   Blocker, Clyde E., Robert H. Plummer, and Richard C. Richardson, Jr. *The Two Year College: A Social Synthesis.* Englewood Cliffs: Prentice-Hall. 1965.

3. An article or reference book

   "Azimuthal Equidistant Projection." *Webster's New Collegiate Dictionary.* 1980 ed.

4. A magazine or a periodical

   Begley, Sharon. "A Healthy Dose of Laughter." *Newsweek.* 4 Oct. 1982.

5. A computer program

   "Alaskan Seals." *Encarta '95.* Microsoft. 1995.

6. An Interview

   Fellini, Federico. "The Long Interview." *Juliet of the Spirits.* Ed., Tullio Kezich. Trans., Howard Greenfield. New York: Ballantine, 1966. 17–64.

The Research Award

presented to

Date

Signed

Acting It Out

Objective

to provide the students with a chance to decide what they would do in certain scenarios that involve a choice of using or not using drugs

Activity

This activity involves three days or three blocks of time. Each activity is designed to be used in the given order with a classroom debate after the first two activities.

Each activity may be reproduced and mounted on index stock for stability. Divide your students into groups and distribute the activity sheets to each group. Allow about 30–40 minutes for the students to write their scripts and to plan their skits. You may wish the students to create scenery. If so, you must allow more time.

Activities

1. Activities One and Two are scenes at a party. Your students are asked to decide what they would do in that given situation. A class discussion should follow each skit.

2. Activity Three is a scene just before the big game. In this case the student is asked what would happen if someone presented him/her with a performance-enhancing drug. Again a class discussion should follow the students' writing session.

3. Debate—divide your class into equal parts. Have one section fight for the right to place stricter controls on the use of drugs. The other section is to fight for the right to legalize the use of all drugs for any purpose. Allow students a week or two to prepare for the debate. Suggest that they go to the local library for research in books, magazines, and news articles. They can make posters, placards, or handouts to support their side of the argument.

   See Rules for Debating after Activity Four (page 161).

What Would You Do?

In this activity you will read about different situations that you might face in the future. If you were confronted with these scenarios, what would you do? Read and complete the questions that follow each scene.

Activity One

You are at the party of the year! All the popular kids at school are there also. Someone spikes the punch, and off in one corner there is a group of kids smoking marijuana. Decide with your group what would be the best solution to this problem. After all, you do not want to be looked down on. Create the dialogue you might say to your friends and the actions you would do to avoid drinking and smoking.

Response

What Would You Do? *(cont.)*

Activity Two

You are at the greatest party of the year. Suddenly you realize that someone has brought a few bottles of alcohol and some six-packs of beer. Things start to get rowdy.

What would you do?

Would you try to stop others from drinking when you realized that the alcohol was brought in?

Would you leave the party, even if your friends wanted to stay?

Would you continue to party and not let the alcohol affect your fun?

Would you try to convince your friends that all of you should leave the party because someone might get hurt?

Should you call the police, explain the situation, and ask for help?

Your skit should depict a group of party goers trying to decide what the right solution to this problem is.

Response

What Would You Do? *(cont.)*

Read the following passage and write your responses. Ask yourself "What if I were in this situation? What actions would I take?"

Activity Three

You decide to try-out for a team. You are chosen for your athletic abilities, but once you are on the team you are offered a legal, performance-enhancing drug before a game.

If you are placed in this situation, would you take the drug? After all, it is legal, and you want to do your best for the team and your school.

What questions might you ask about the drug before you take it?

What if everyone on the team is taking the drug except you?

What if you are the team's star player and are expected to carry the team to victory? Would you take the drug?

What if it meant the difference between your team winning a state championship and perhaps losing it?

After responding individually, divide your group in half to debate this question in front of the class. One side is to argue for taking the drug, and the other is to argue against the drugs. Include in your debate factual information from various sources. Allow time for class discussion afterwards.

Response

What Would You Do? *(cont.)*

Activity Four

You are at your locker and you spot a student taking a calculator out of another student's backpack. Do you say nothing to the student, or do you approach and tell him/her that you saw what was done? Do you go the principal or a teacher to report what you saw? Do you call the police? Write a short play about this scenario. Present it to the class. Feel free to add any other choices you may think of.

Response

Rules for Debating

1. Opening Statements

An opening statement occurs when each side states what its subject is and what it is going to cover in the arguments.

The PRO team is the first to present their opening statement.

The CON presents their opening statement after the PRO team.

2. Statement of Facts

The statement of facts is the argument presented by the debaters that tries to persuade the audience to see things their way.

PRO—statement of facts

CON—statement of facts

3. Rebuttal

The rebuttal consists of the PRO and CON follow-up comments on one another's cases.

PRO—Comments in answer to the CON'S arguments

CON—Comments in answer to the PRO's arguments

4. Closing Statement

The closing statement consists of the final comments from each side, intended to sway the audience to their way of thinking.

5. Open Discussion

The open discussion is an audience participation time. This allows everyone to voice individual opinions on the issues presented.

6. Judging (Optional)

The judging is a statement from a panel of selected students as to which side presented a more convincing argument. The panel of judges should consist of four to five students who are capable of keeping open minds throughout the debate and then deciding on which side of the debate was more convincing.

Debate Summary Sheet

Use the following sheet to write your arguments, pro and con, as you are watching the debate. And then after you reflect on what has been said after the class discussion, write your own comments and conclusions about the matter

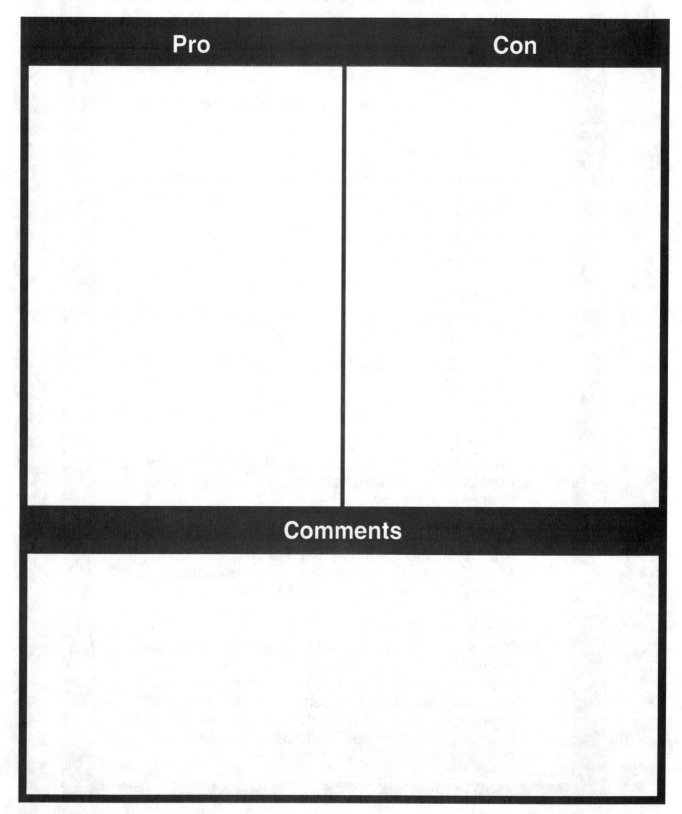

Pro	Con

Comments

Gangs

Objective

To make students aware of what gangs are and why some people join them

Background

With the changes in family structure that have taken place in recent years, many children do not experience a tightly structured home environment. In many cases both parents work, and the children are cared for by relatives or baby sitters. In many cases there is only a single-parent household. In some cases there is no adult supervision at all during the hours after school until a parent arrives home from work. It is during these hours that children are dangerously vulnerable to the pressure of peers.

Gangs often become a kind of substitute family for some children, and they tend to flourish most in areas where both parents are working until evening or in single-parent homes. Most gang-related activities occur where the family is weakest. Conversely, most group-related activities with responsible adult supervision—e.g., Boy Scouts, Girl Scouts, Campfire Girls, YMCA, YWCA, and YMHA—seem to flourish where the family structure is the strongest. Understanding the dynamics of gang attraction is paramount for middle school students today, if for no other reason than for self-defense.

Activity

1. Display various Norman Rockwell pictures depicting the family. Include pictures from magazines of present-day families. Show the pictures to the class in no special order.

2. Elicit from the class what they think might be the differences between the families of yesterday and the families of today.

3. Have the students complete the following activity sheet (page 164). Under each heading, have them list what they think are appropriate characteristics, including those developed in the previous discussion.

4. Ask the students to write what factors they think caused the family to change over the years. Do they feel the change was for the better or for the worse?

5. Have the students bring in newspapers for the next part of this lesson (page 165).

Gangs *(cont.)*

Families of Yesterday	Families of Today

What factors do you think led to family changes over the years?

_____

_____

_____

Do you feel these changes have been for the better or the worse? Why?

_____

_____

_____

Families and Gangs

Look in the newspaper for any stories mentioning families. Write the title of the article and give a short description of what the story is about.

_____

_____

_____

_____

_____

If your story involves a crime, was it gang related? In what ways?

_____

_____

_____

_____

Continue to look through the newspaper and tally the numbers of stories that revolve around the family that are gang or crime related and the numbers of stories of families that are happy and have achieved positive goals or accomplishments.

Stories that are negative about the family: _____

_____

_____

Stories that are positive about the family: _____

_____

_____

What do you think are the reasons for your results?

_____

_____

_____

_____

Gangs *(cont.)*

As you have seen, the family has changed a great deal. It used to be that Mom almost always stayed home with the children and Dad went to work. Today we see a change in that pattern. True, in some cases, that situation remains the same, but in most cases both parents work and the children are cared for by an aunt, grandparent, or baby sitter. In some cases, there is no adult supervision at all until dinner time. It is during the hours after school until the parent arrives home that children are most vulnerable to the pressures of their peers. This is a dangerous time, for all children need the steady judgment and guidance of concerned adults, preferably those nearest and dearest to them—the family.

Gangs are a kind of substitute family for some children, and they tend to flourish most in areas where both parents are working until the evening or in one-parent families. Therefore, most gang-related activities occur where the family is the weakest.

Some "gangs" are nothing more than groups of young people sharing common interests, but we do not label these groups "gangs." They are clubs like the YMCA or the Boy Scouts or Girl Scouts. Such youth groups are under the direct supervision of caring adults, and they flourish where the family structure tends to be the strongest.

The term "gang" has a negativity associated with it. When we think of a gang, we usually think of crime, drugs, and violence. This is true whether one lives in the North, South, East, or West. Gangs and crime just go together.

Information Please!

Do some investigation on your own. Find out about gang life and crime. Write a report for your class of your findings. Then present this to the class. Begin the report in the space below and continue it on the back of this page.

Conflict Resolution

Working It Out!

Student conflicts that might end in violence are becoming an increasing problem on many school campuses. Many of our young adolescents come from homes where the first response to a problem is the threat of physical force. In today's newspapers and magazines, our impressionable students are bombarded with violence as the solution to problems.

Students need to realize that open communication and reasoning can solve most problems without the need for violence. The following pages present your students with activities that will enable them to resolve their conflicts without the physical contact.

Activity

1. Use the activity sheets that follow to introduce your students to conflict resolution. They may be used as a week's activity or a weekly activity over the quarter.

   It might to helpful to introduce conflict resolution skills throughout the quarter if your students are not physical in problem solving. On the other hand, starting with these activities at the beginning of the quarter is very effective for physical students.

2. Throughout the rest of the quarter or semester, it will be helpful to review these skills with either type of groups.

CONFLICT SITUATION

Reason for Conflict

Possible Solutions

3. When the students have completed each activity sheet, a follow-up discussion should be held. It is important for the students to be able to air their views and their solutions to their conflicts. It is also important for students to hear that other students have similar problems and learn what their solutions are.

The discussion section allows students to learn new coping and resolution skills.

Conflict Resolution *(cont.)*

Activity One

1. Look for the word *conflict* in the dictionary and write the definition below.

_____

_____

2. What are some examples of conflict that you have found in your life?

_____

_____

3. What are some of the ways you have solved your conflicts?

_____

_____

4. The experience of talking, thinking, and writing down what bothers you is one way of peacefully ending conflicts. Find someone you enjoy talking to and share your responses with questions 1–3. See if talking with another person might provide better solutions than the ones you used. Write your responses below.

_____

_____

_____

_____

_____

Thinking Ahead

Think about the skills you would need to negotiate and compromise.

Write them below.

_____

_____

_____

_____

_____

_____

Conflict Resolution *(cont.)*

Activity Two

Think back to the last time you had a disagreement or an argument with someone. It might have been a friend, a brother, a sister, or a parent. Write the name of the person below and your relationship with that person. Then write what the conflict was and how it was resolved.

_____

_____

_____

_____

Was the resolution or end of the conflict satisfactory to you or to the other person?

_____

_____

_____

What kinds of conflict do you often become involved in—adult/child, child/child, parent/child, individual/group, or group/group?

Examine your feelings about each of these conflict pairs and explain them below.

_____

_____

_____

_____

Thinking Ahead

Write a list of the ways in which you have resolved conflicts. Check the ones that have worked best for you.

_____

_____

_____

_____

_____

Conflict Resolution *(cont.)*

Activity Three

Look back at Activity Two and re-read the list of ways that you resolved conflicts.

You must know after the discussions you have had in class that there are many ways to resolve conflicts. Whatever manner you used, conflict is the struggle to have one's goals met. Sometimes that struggle succeeds, and in other cases it fails. Feelings get hurt, and everyone is usually upset. Look at the various ways to resolve conflicts and see which ones are most helpful to you.

Win/Lose

In the win/lose situation, one person gets resolution or satisfaction to the conflict, and the other comes up short. This can also be called the "either/or" conflict. Like playing a game, there is a winner and a loser. The rules of the game are clear. Power is the most distinguishing characteristic of the win/lose conflict. Power can be either physical or one of position.

For example:

- *Parent/Child:* Have your parents ever threatened you with physical power? Have they ever said, "Stop that or I'll send you to your room!"? or "Touch that again and I'll break your arms!"?

- *Teacher/Student:* In this case the outcome is always predictable. The student is the loser. Teachers use the power of grades as a tool to get students to behave in desired ways.

- *Employer/Employee:* Obviously the employee is the loser. The employer is the person who has all the authority and can fire or hire.

- *David/Goliath:* In this relationship, the size of Goliath made him appear to be the probable winner in this conflict, but that was not the outcome. David used his courage, wit, intelligence, and skill with a sling to outsmart the oversized giant. Courage, intellect, mental power, and special skills can also be tools for a win/lose relationship.

In all of the above situations there are clear-cut winners and losers. Sometimes the win/lose technique is the best way to solve conflicts. When we vote and do what the majority feels is best, we have a win/lose situation. No matter how fair the outcome is, there is still a loser. Another type of win/lose situation occurs when one party to a conflict insists on defeating the other and no other solution is apparent—such as someone wanting to inflict bodily harm or a criminal deliberately breaking the law.

Conflict Resolution *(cont.)*

Lose/Lose

In the lose/lose situation, neither party is satisfied with the outcome. Compromise is the tool in the lose/lose situation. Both parties are willing to settle for less than they want because they feel that this is the best answer to the problem. Wars are a good example of the lose/lose situation. Both sides suffer loss of lives, loss of land, or loss of power. There is really no victory in war.

On a personal level, the individuals usually lose pride, and both subjects suffer.

Win/Win

Just as the name implies, the outcome of this type of conflict is quite different from the others. The results of this situation are that there are two winners, and both parties' needs are satisfied. The goal of the win/win conflict is to seek a solution that satisfies the needs of everyone involved. Working together to solve problems and reach goals is a good way to satisfy both parties.

Following is one example of a win/win resolution:

You hold a job after school. You have exams and ask your boss for time off to study. He says he is short handed and cannot give you time off. You discuss various solutions to the problem, but none is agreeable to both parties. Finally it is suggested that you trade hours with another employee so that you can study. Both parties are happy.

The win/win approach works only when each of the persons involved in the conflict cares about the relationship and is interested in helping the other as well as himself.

Conflict Resolution *(cont.)*

Think about how you have solved problems in the past. Do you think they could have been resolved in a better manner than in the one that was used?

Describe some of your conflicts and tell how you resolved them. Choose one of the methods of resolving conflicts and explain how they might have better resolved your conflict.

_____

_____

_____

_____

_____

_____

_____

_____

_____

_____

_____

_____

_____

_____

_____

_____

_____

_____

_____

_____

_____

_____

_____

_____

Conflict Resolution Techniques

Try These to Solve Your Conflicts, and Everyone Is a Winner!

1. Think about the conflicts and state your needs.

Be clear about your needs. Speak with another person if you are unsure about what you desire.

2. Share your needs with the other person.

Choose a time and place to discuss your needs with the other person. Try to use the "I" word when stating what you desire.

3. Listen carefully to the other person's needs.

Listen carefully and without interrupting. It is important to understand what the other person's needs are.

4. Think of possible solutions to the conflict.

Brainstorming or inventing various ways can solve problems. Sometimes another person's idea can spark a solution to a problem.

5. Evaluate the solutions.

Review the lists of solutions with the other person. Do they satisfy both person's needs? Will everyone be a winner? Choose the best solution for both of you.

6. Implement the solution.

Finding a solution to a problem is not any good if you do not follow it through. Both parties must make an effort to see that the conflict does not again rear its ugly head!

(Reproduce this poster and hang it up in your room.)

Conflict Resolution *(cont.)*

Author Shel Silverstein said it best in *Where the Sidewalk Ends*. Perhaps you have read his book of poems or have heard it read.

Read the poem "Tug O' War" to your class or have one of your students read the poem and experience Silverstein's version of the win/win resolution.

Have your students create their own poems that reflect the various stages of conflict. These poems can then be mounted and pictures from magazines can be used to depict what they are saying, or you might have your more artistic students do the drawing for you.

Sample Poster

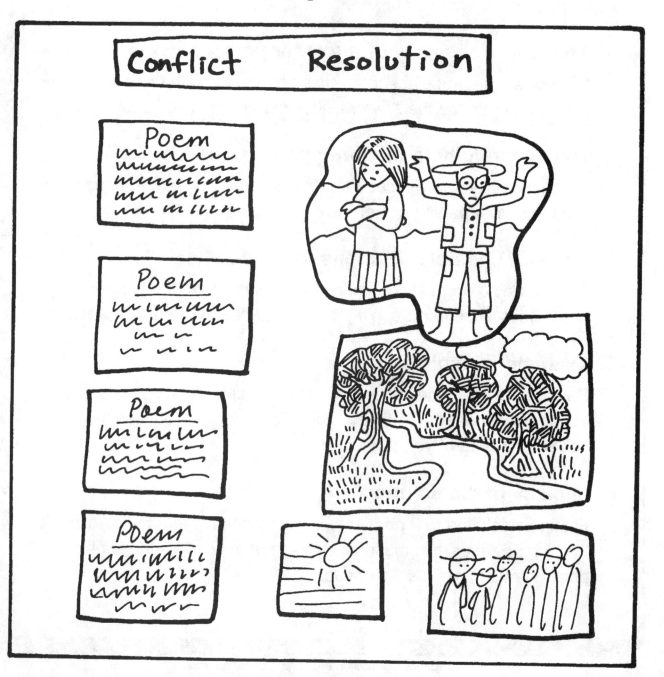

Conflict Resolution *(cont.)*

Peaceful Heroes

Objective

to give students an opportunity to see peaceful resolution to conflicts

Materials:

- several sheets of butcher paper
- crayons, markers, or paint

Activity

1. Divide your class into several groups, three to four students each.

2. Explain to the class that there are many literary and mythical heroes who resolve their conflicts peacefully. Such heroes and heroines appear widely in the mythology and folklore of many cultures. Begin the class discussion with the following literary heroes or heroines that may be familiar to them. Ask what qualities each character possessed that made him/her a peaceful hero.

Literary Heroes

- Belle—*The Beauty and the Beast*
- Cinderella—*Cinderella*
- Androcles—*Androcles and the Lion*
- Gulliver—*Gulliver's Travels*

Historical Heroes

- Mohammed
- Gandhi
- Moses
- Confucius

Have the students research the literary characters they have read about in social studies or in English that might fit the role of a peaceful hero. There are even literary heroes in comic books, so allow your students to explore all avenues available to them. (Most conventional comic book heroes, of course, are far from being "peaceful.")

3. After your students have researched their literary heroes, have them draw the hero's picture on the I Admire activity sheet and have them choose one attribute that they admire about that hero.

4. Brainstorm with your class to find some of characters or real persons that they feel capture the meaning of being "Peaceful Heroes" and draw their pictures on the butcher paper.

5. Draw dialogue bubbles and use them to explain the skill your characters might use to resolve conflict.

6. Color your mural in an eye-catching manner.

7. Display your mural in your room to remind your students that fighting is not the best way to settle conflict.

I Admire . . .

Draw a picture of the literary or historical hero or heroine that you admire most. At the bottom of the page, explain why you have chosen this person and what you admire about this person.

176

Goal Setting

Objective

to keep students focused during the last quarter of school before summer vacation

(Fourth quarter is usually the time students begin to lose their focus about school and begin to make plans for the summer. It is important for the teacher to keep the students focused when setting their goals. For most eighth grade teachers, this task also involves readying the students for high school.

Activity

1. Instruct each student to make a list of goals for fourth quarter.

2. Ask them to include in their goals ways they can keep their effort and interest level high.

3. Discuss these goals as a class and decide on a few to become classroom, as well as individual, goals.

4. Construct a classroom Goals Chart listing four or five of the central goals chosen by the class. Post this in a prominent place in the room.

5. Follow this activity with another goals list consisting of a series of individual goals—a personal goal chosen by each student in class for himself or herself and signed. These are each to be written on separate strips of white construction paper and posted around the room. They may be stretched around the room in a long series or grouped appropriately on one bulletin board, to remain there as reminders and motivators during the fourth quarter.

6. On Monday of each week, make a practice of reviewing the class and individual goals. It is a good idea to ask each student in turn to suggest a specific action to take that week in order to further progress toward his/her stated goal(s). Do this orally.

   Monday seems a better day than Friday for this activity because it is the beginning of a school week and tends to focus effort on fresh beginnings, rather than serving as a kind of summing up of work completed or perhaps left undone. The function of this activity is really akin to that of a pep rally, encouraging individual effort by enlisting the group to cheer on each person in turn. The class becomes a team seeking unified success.

7. Many teachers find that extra effort on their part is necessary to keep student interest elevated through the end of the school year, but the effort is worthwhile.

Goal-Setting *(cont.)*

Think about the things that worked and did not work well for you so far this year and write them below.

- What worked well?

  _____

  _____

  _____

- What did not work well?

  _____

  _____

  _____

- How can I change what did not work well for me?

  _____

  _____

  _____

- What are those things that I learned about in class that I can use in the fourth quarter?

  _____

  _____

  _____

- How can I change my habits and thoughts to make myself a better student and person?

  _____

  _____

  _____

- What goals would I like to accomplish in the fourth quarter?

  _____

  _____

  _____

- What improvements do I still need to make in the future?

  _____

  _____

Fourth Quarter

Life Skills

- Perseverance
- Effort
- Problem Solving
- Curiosity

Multicultural Activities
Goal Setting

Working Out Problems

Objective

to gain insight into how others settle problems and how to implement such skills for oneself

(In this activity the students should view the problems they encounter as challenges to conquer rather than obstacles or threats that will conquer them. Working through problems, the students gain insight into how others settle problems and how they can implement those skills for themselves.)

Activity

1. Set the scene for the students by asking them if they have ever heard these expressions:

   I feel as if I'm carrying a ton of bricks.
   I have a heavy heart.
   That's a load off my mind.
   I feel as if I've been stabbed in the heart.

2. These expressions are used when people describe something that is not right. Problems often overwhelm us to the point that we cannot concentrate on anything else. Problems can interfere with our general well-being to the extent that we become consumed by them.

3. Elicit from your students the ways that they solve their problems. Do they talk to a friend about them? Do they seek the advice of an adult, such as a parent or teacher? Do they try to work them out for themselves, or do they do nothing?

4. Students need to realize that problems do not go away and that help is sometimes needed to resolve them.

5. Copy That's a Load off My Mind activity sheet for each of your students.

6. Have them complete the activity sheets, but caution them that their answers will be shared with their classmates.

7. Share the students' responses and allow them to develop a plan to solve problems.

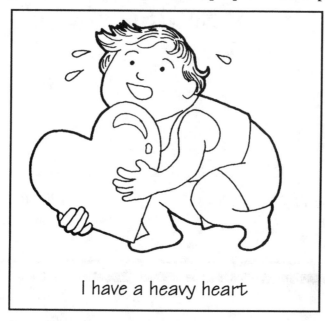

I have a heavy heart

180

That's a Load off My Mind

Step 1

The first step in solving a problem is to admit that you have one.

My problem is . . .

(Write your problem here.)

_____

Step 2

My problem affects the following people:

(List those people.)

_____

Step 3

What are some of the ways I can solve my problem?

_____

Step 4

I would ask the following people for their help in solving my problem:

_____

Step 5

I would like to share my problem with the following person(s):

My friend _____

My parents _____

My counselor _____

My classmate _____

What would you say? _____

_____

_____

_____

The philosopher Epicharmus once wrote:

A wise man must be wise before, not after, the event.

Knowing how to solve your problems before they happen lessens the severity of the problem when it occurs.

It's a Problem for Me

Objective
to provide students a chance to become better problem solvers by solving problems

Introduction
We do not live in a vacuum. Ethical problems most commonly involve our interactions with other people or with our consciences. The more a person is exposed to interactive problems, the better equipped the person becomes at dealing with these situations.

The first activities ready your students to think in different ways. The simple problems help the students to realize that not everyone solves problems in the same way. Knowing that there is no single one-two-three solution to problem solving nor is there but a single method of thought and reasoning—that is the key to this process.

The second group of activities are some real life situations that your students might face in their lives. Once again, these situations all require the students to use thought, reasoning, and awareness of one's conscience.

Activities
1. Copy the following pages for your students. Note: These pages may be used alone or as daily activities over a few days.

2. After each activity sheet, remember to debrief the class and thoroughly discuss the work completed.

Above and Beyond enables students to see the limitations of their preconceived thinking.

Visual Image provides the students the opportunity to solve problems in different ways. Sharing the ways each of your students solves this problem allows the students to see that not everyone solves problems in the same way.

Can You Solve This? (Activity One) requires the students to experiment with a trial-and-error method of problem solving. The manipulation of the shapes makes use of a visual pattern for this method.

Can You Solve This? (Activity Two) enables the students to realize that some problems can be solved in ways that are different from the normal problem-solving steps.

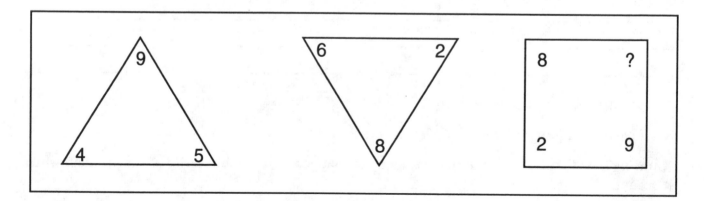

It's a Problem for Me *(cont.)*

Solutions to the Problems

Above and Beyond (page 184)

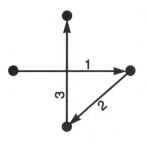

Visual Image (page 186)

Possible Responses: F, B, W, M, 3, Triangle

Can You Solve This? (Activity One—page 188)

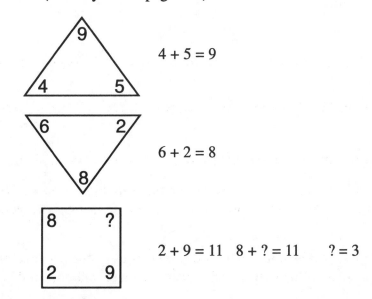

$4 + 5 = 9$

$6 + 2 = 8$

$2 + 9 = 11$ $8 + ? = 11$ $? = 3$

The answer is three. Explanation: The sum of the numbers at the base of each triangle is equal to the total sum at the tip. Therefore, the sum of the numbers at the base of the square $(2 + 9 = 11)$ should equal the sum of the numbers at the top of the square $(8 + ? = 11)$ or 3.

Can You Solve This? (Activity Two—page 189)

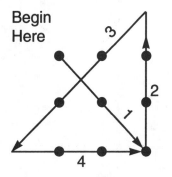

It's a Problem for Me *(cont.)*

Above and Beyond

The challenge of this puzzle is to connect all five dots of the diamond, using three straight lines. You may not lift your pencil from the paper or retrace a line. If you have to lift your pencil or retrace a line, you need to start over again.

If you finish early, turn your paper over and write down the steps you used to solve the problem.

Do not be discouraged if you keep trying and do not solve the problem. Try to go about it again, but try to think of a different way to solve it.

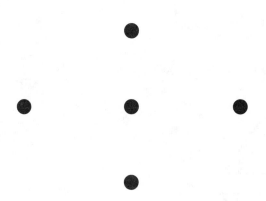

Now try to draw this house without lifting your pencil.

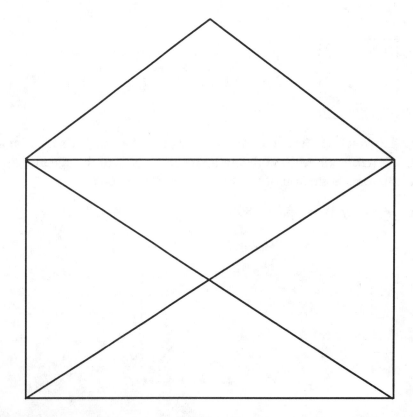

184

It's a **Problem for Me** *(cont.)*

Above and Beyond *(cont.)*

Answer the following questions fully.

1. How did you approach this problem?

   _____

   _____

   _____

2. When you found out that you could not solve the problem one way, what did you do?

   _____

   _____

3. Are there times in your life when things did not work out for you? Did you continue to do things in the same way, or did you change them? If you changed them, what did you do?

   _____

   _____

   _____

4. Was there something that prevented you from changing things?

   _____

   _____

   _____

5. Has this problem been affecting other areas of your life? How?

   _____

   _____

   _____

6. Did you try to ask for some help in solving this problem? If you answered no, why not?

   _____

   _____

   _____

7. Think of the different approaches to problem solving that you have learned about this year. What approaches do you think might help you solve your problem? You may share your problem with the class during our discussion time. Perhaps our class can be of some help.

   _____

   _____

   _____

It's a Problem for Me *(cont.)*

Visual Image

Sometimes we see certain situations in different ways from other people. Look carefully at the picture below for one minute. Can you recognize it?

Beside the image, write your thoughts on what it could be.

Identify this object:

186

It's a Problem for Me *(cont.)*

Visual Image *(cont.)*

If you still have no idea what the image on the previous page could be, here is a hint. This is an extremely common image that has been masked so that it is not easy to recognize.

Now write below what ideas you have about the image.

_____

_____

_____

_____

_____

_____

_____

_____

_____

_____

_____

_____

_____

_____

_____

_____

_____

_____

Sometimes a person needs to stand back and take a different view of one's problems; so turn the image in all directions and see if you can identify the image now.

The image is _____ .

It's a Problem for Me *(cont.)*

Can You Solve This? (Activity One)

Below you will find two triangles and a square. Carefully study the relationship between the numbers in each of the triangles. Explain the relationship below.

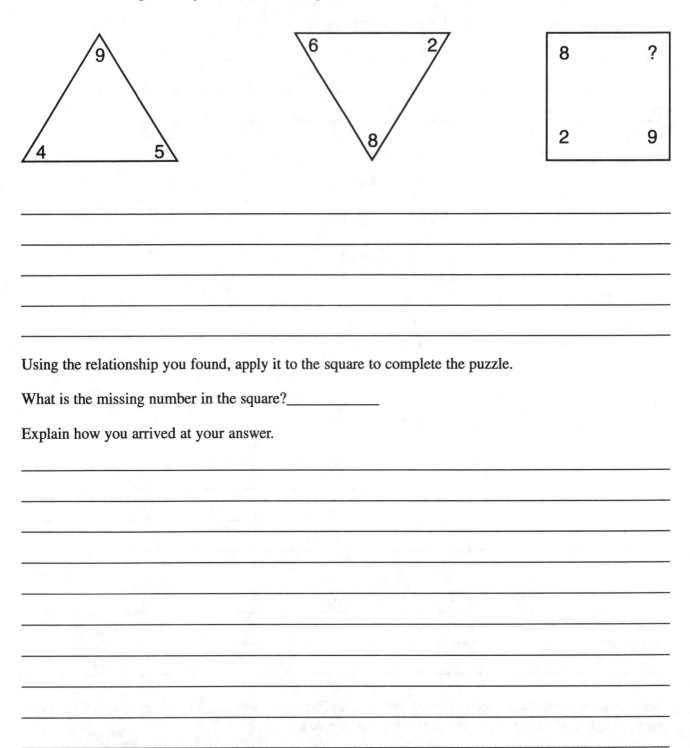

_____

_____

_____

_____

_____

Using the relationship you found, apply it to the square to complete the puzzle.

What is the missing number in the square?_____

Explain how you arrived at your answer.

_____

_____

_____

_____

_____

_____

_____

_____

_____

It's a Problem for Me *(cont.)*

Can You Solve This? (Activity Two)

Starting from any point you wish but without lifting your pencil or retracing a line, join together all the dots on this page, using four straight lines only.

●   ●   ●

●   ●   ●

●   ●   ●

The Problem Solving Award

presented to

Eureka!

Date

Signed

Real Life Problems

Not all problems are like the ones you solved in previous activities. Some of the problems we solve are about real life situations. Some of the problems we face in life are problems that we have no control over. However, if you role play situations about real life problems, you develop skills to use if you are ever faced with similar situations.

The activities that you are going to complete now are possible problems that you might have to solve in the future.

Many times your friends put pressure on you to do something that you know is wrong, but you do it anyway. This is called *peer pressure*. People, children and adults alike, give in to peer pressure because of the need to be "liked or accepted" as part of the group.

If you or your friends find others putting pressure on you to do something, remember the following:

1. Make the decision on your own about what to do and stick to it.

2. Stand by your decision; be confident in your decision.

3. Do not let your friends persuade you to do what is wrong.

4. Remind your friends of the possible trouble you might get into.

5. Suggest another activity for everyone to do.

6. Walk away from the situation. If you cannot change the minds of your friends, let them go their own way and be confident that you have made the right choice.

7. If you know that your friends are going to do something that is serious or someone might get hurt, get help.

I Am Innocent

There are times when you might get in trouble when someone else does something wrong and you are with them. Failure to resist harmful situations can be just as bad as cooperating. Complete the following situations by writing your own conclusions.

Situation One

You are with your friends. One of them throws a rock at a passing car and breaks the window. The car stops and everybody runs. But the driver of the car is your neighbor, and she recognizes you.

_____

_____

_____

_____

_____

_____

_____

_____

_____

Situation Two

You are at a party given by your friends. Their parents are away for the weekend. Someone brings alcohol, and everyone is smoking. The doorbell rings. It is the police. Some neighbors called them because of the noise the party created.

_____

_____

_____

_____

_____

_____

I Am Innocent *(cont.)*

Situation Three

You go to the mall with your best friend. You go into the music store to look at some CD's. The manager of the store notices that your friend has put a CD into his jacket pocket, but the manager does nothing at this time. You and your friend purchase a CD and try to leave the store when the manager stops the both of you and takes the CD from your friend's pocket.

_____

_____

_____

_____

_____

_____

_____

_____

_____

Situation Four

You are visiting a friend's house. Your friend takes you up to her parent's bedroom to show you her father's gun hidden in a drawer. As you pick up the gun, your friend's father walks into the room.

_____

_____

_____

_____

_____

_____

_____

_____

Are You Doing the Right Thing?

Sometimes in life you may find yourself in circumstances that you can control. These situations are often a matter of conscience. Conscience is that little voice inside you that tells you right from wrong. It can also advise you on many life situations if you give it a chance.

Situation A

Suppose you one day see your neighbor discipline his dog by kicking it and beating it with a rod. What would be the right thing to do?

_____

_____

_____

_____

_____

_____

_____

_____

_____

_____

_____

_____

_____

_____

_____

_____

_____

_____

_____

_____

Are You Doing the **Right Thing ?** *(cont.)*

Situation B

You are part of the "in" group in your school. One of the less popular students confides in you that he/she has not been able to make any real friends. This person asks you to help him/her make friends, but your friends are against the idea. What is your decision?

_____

_____

_____

_____

_____

_____

_____

_____

_____

_____

Situation C

You are in the store paying for your purchases. The sales clerk gives you twice as much change as you are supposed to receive. What do you do next?

_____

_____

_____

_____

_____

_____

_____

_____

_____

_____

Are You Doing the Right Thing ? *(cont.)*

Situation D

It is two weeks before finals, and everyone is nervous about the math test. One of your friends confides in you that he/she has "obtained" a copy of the final. Some of the students are getting together to study this copy of the test next week. Do you go, or do you stay?

_____

_____

_____

_____

_____

_____

_____

_____

_____

Situation E

You are taking a test. The teacher leaves the room for a few moments. Your best friend asks to see your answers. You know that he/she did not study and is not prepared for the test. You, on the other hand, have studied long and hard over a few weeks of time. Does your friend get to see your answers? How do you think you would feel if your friend received a better grade?

_____

_____

_____

_____

_____

_____

_____

_____

Are You Doing the Right Thing ? *(cont.)*

Situation F

You have been invited to a party, but your parents do not allow you to go because there will be no parent supervision. All the best people will be there. You feel like a baby and are miserable because your parents do not trust you. What do you do? You decide to lie to your parents and tell them you are staying over at a friend's house. You go to the party, but it is crashed by some rowdy kids and things get out of hand. You cannot call your friend because he knows nothing about your lie and it is too late to call anyway. What do you do and why?

_____

_____

_____

_____

_____

_____

_____

Situation G

You are in class and your class is taking a major test. You glance over at one of your classmates and see that he/she is cheating. You say nothing. You have studied and are confident that you will do well on the test. However, when the tests are returned you find that the cheater received an A and you only earned a C. What do you do? Do you remain quiet, or do you go to the teacher? What are the pros and cons of each situation?

_____

_____

_____

_____

_____

_____

_____

Are You Doing the Right Thing ? *(cont.)*

Situation H

You are baby-sitting at a neighbor's home. The children are sound asleep, and curiosity gets the best of you. You begin to investigate the rooms in the house. In the master bedroom you find a $50.00 bill lying on the floor by the dresser. It is obvious that it was dropped unknowingly. Do you leave the bill where it is? Do you pick it up and put it on the dresser? Do you take it because the owner would not know what happened to it and you can use the extra money? Think of all the ramifications that might happen in each situation. Is there anything else you could do? What is the right thing to do?

_____

_____

_____

_____

_____

_____

_____

_____

_____

_____

_____

_____

_____

_____

_____

_____

_____

_____

Looking Toward the Future

Many of your students have a strong sense of self at this age and might be making plans about what college to go to or what career they desire after high school. What activities can you provide to help them strengthen their views or help them decide a career path to take?

Walking Down Life's Path (page 200) encourages your students to look toward the future. Most of the young people today do not look far enough into the future. They see things from week to week, but most do not realize that the actions of today affect the outcomes of tomorrow.

Fame and Fortune (pages 201–202) allows students to explore possibilities for a future job and the preparation that is necessary for the job. This activity allows the students to visualize themselves in that role.

After I'm Gone . . . (pages 204–205) is a very futuristic look at how persons might want others to remember them. Students are asked to project themselves into the future after they have departed this world. They are looking down on the Earth and listening to what people are saying about them. From letters, journals, and stories written by the student, the world gets to know them.

My Family Tree (page 206) is an intriguing activity for the students. Here they get to investigate their roots. A family tree shows the family lineage and background information obtained from older family members.

My Past, Present, and Future (page 207) is a personal time line of the student's life. Major firsts and special events are included in this lifeline. The third section is creative. The student is asked to create his/her future.

Walking Down Life's Path

Think about the future—not the near future, but 20 years into the future. Just imagine how things have changed. Think about how you have changed.

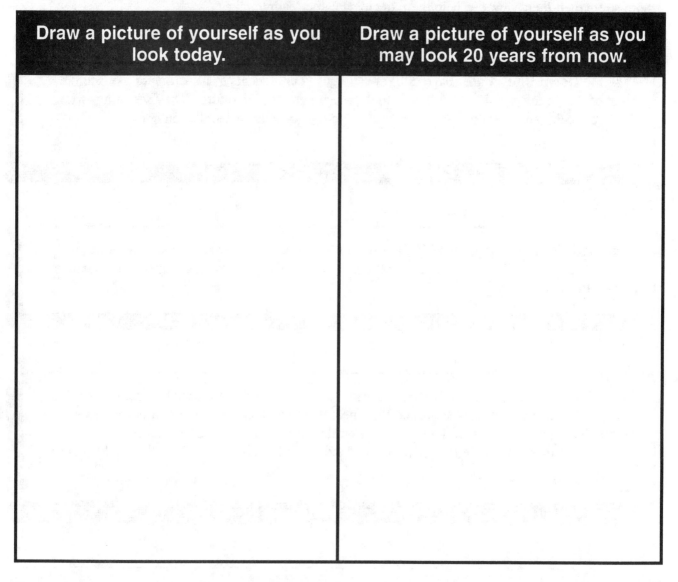

Draw a picture of yourself as you look today.	Draw a picture of yourself as you may look 20 years from now.

On another sheet of paper, describe what the world is like and what you are like. Consider the following guidelines:

  a. Describe yourself physically.

  b. Describe your job.

  c. Describe your family life.

  d. Describe your lifestyle.

  e. Describe your value system.

(Include a description of what the world looks like—the types of houses and new inventions that are household gadgets.)

Fame and Fortune

Even though students are still in middle school (or on their way to high school), it is not too early to start thinking about what they desire in the future and what skills they might need to get there. Students often say, "What do I need algebra (or fill in the subject of your choice) for? Am I ever gonna use this stuff?"

It is surprising how many activities do use algebraic skills and the many other skills that are learned in school.

Ask them to think about what they might want to do in the future. Ask them to remember that they are the controllers of their own destinies, and they are capable of doing much to achieve their desires.

Activity

The activity sheet on the following page will guide the students in their thoughts about their future. They will answer the following.

1. Write down a career that you would like to pursue when you are grown.

2. Describe what you think your responsibilities would be when doing this job.

3. What requirements do you think you need to get the job?

4. What skills or schooling does this job require?

Put this paper in a safe place and do the following.

1. Look through the local phone book and find someone who works in the profession you have chosen.

2. Call that person and explain that you are doing research on careers and you would like information about what they do and what skills you might need to do this job.

3. It is best if you can make an appointment to speak to this person personally or at a convenient time. After all, people are busy, and this might not be a good time for that person.

4. Make a list of important questions for you to ask at your meeting.

5. When you go to the meeting, be sure to dress neatly and be very polite. Try to make a good impression.

6. Bring a pencil and paper with you so that you can make notes.

7. When you return to school, write a thank-you note stating that you appreciate the time spent with you and the helpful information you received.

8. Review your notes and write the information on the career choice page.

9. Present your career choice to your class.

10. Take out that sheet of paper and compare what you thought your career choice was about with what it is actually about. Did you realize all that your career entails?

Fame and Fortune *(cont.)*

Student Reflections Sheet

Carefully think about the following questions before you write them on your paper.

1. Write down a career that you would like to pursue when you are grown.

   _____

   _____

   _____

2. Describe what you think your responsibilities will be when doing this job.

   _____

   _____

   _____

3. What requirements do you think you will need to get the job?

   _____

   _____

   _____

4. What skills or schooling does this job require?

   _____

   _____

   _____

5. Why do you think that this is the career for you?

   _____

   _____

   _____

6. Do you think that this is something you can do for your entire working years until 65, or do you think you may need to make a career change? If so, what might you do?

   _____

   _____

My Career Choice

- In the future I would like to be . . .

_____

- The skills I need to do this job are . . .

_____

_____

_____

- In order to do my job, I need to learn the following subjects:

_____   _____

_____   _____

_____   _____

_____   _____

- It will take me _____ years to learn all that is necessary for me to start working in my career.
- After learning about my career, my thoughts about my career choice have (changed, not changed). Write your response below and explain your feelings.

_____

_____

_____

_____

_____

_____

_____

_____

_____

_____

After I Am Gone

History is often recorded in books, letters, articles, and journals. Most families do not have written records of their history. Most families tell their history by word of mouth. An elder family member often tells the younger members of the family about what it was like when they were young.

Think of a time when you may no longer be living. Your grandchildren are in the attic of your house, and they find your old trunk filled with letters and journals that you have written. In them you relate what your life was like.

Consider the following questions. Put yourself in the future, use your imagination, and write your responses to the following questions. Use the back of this paper if you need more space.

1. What do you want your grandchildren to know and remember about you?

   _____

2. What was your life like when you were growing up?

   _____

3. What activities did you like to do for fun?

   _____

4. What was it like in school?

   _____

5. What special talents or skills did you have?

   _____

6. What were some of your accomplishments that you want your grandchildren to know?

   _____

7. What were some of your adventures?

   _____

8. Who are some of your friends and what did you do together?

   _____

9. What were your parents like?

   _____

10. How did they influence you when you were growing up?

    _____

11. What important decisions did you have to make during your lifetime?

    _____

After I Am Gone *(cont.)*

After you have written your story, interview an elder whom you may know. It could be your own grandparents, an aunt or uncle, cousin, or even a neighbor. Ask this person the same things you wrote about in your story. Compare their responses to the things you wrote.

Now . . . let's make you 75 years old.

Look back on your life and decide what was most important to you in life.

goals

_____

_____

_____

education

_____

_____

_____

accomplishments

_____

_____

_____

people

_____

_____

_____

events

_____

_____

_____

decisions

_____

_____

_____

Explain why you chose those points.

My Family Tree

Complete the family tree. Ask your parents and grandparents for the information if you do not know it yourself.

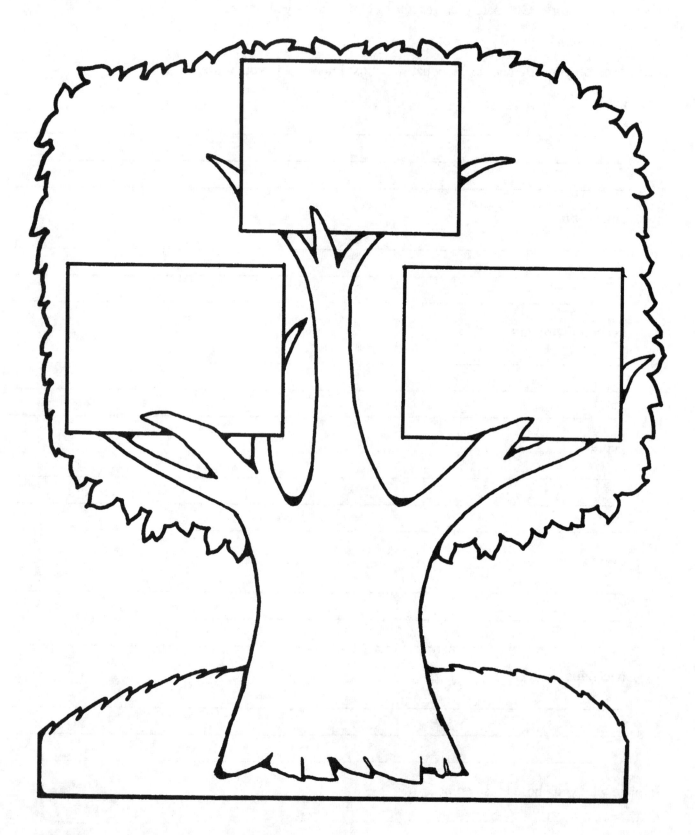

My Past, Present, and Future

Create a personal time line of the important events in your life. Begin with your date of birth and continue to the present day.

Include things like the following:

- first tooth
- first word
- when you learned to walk
- when you learned to ride a bike
- beginning school

- special events in life
- trips
- lessons
- sports
- accomplishments

Although some of you may have many important happenings to remember, limit yourself to the top twenty events.

Then divide a 16" x 20" (40 cm x 50 cm) sheet of white construction paper into 20 boxes and draw each event in each box. Also put the date of the event and the event itself into the box.

Sample Time Line

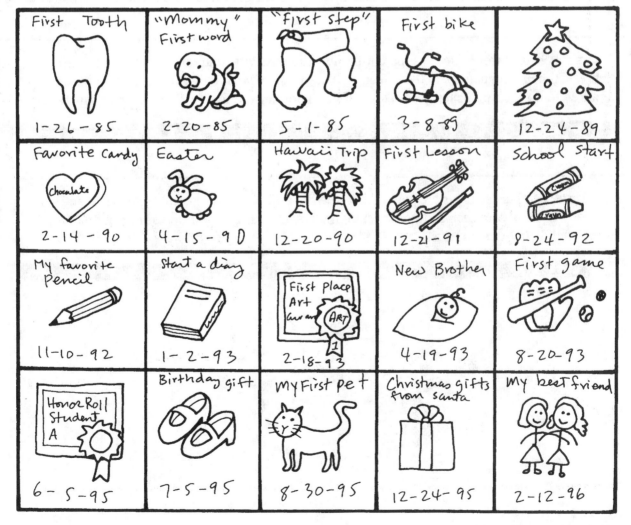

Career Orientation and Planning

Career planning gives students direction for social and emotional progress and development. Planning aids the students in selecting careers that are best suited for their capabilities. Providing activities that expose the students to various career choices enables them to develop realistic goals about their own careers.

Want Ads involves the students in a job search. They peruse the newspaper classified ads to find jobs that they might want to select as career choices. Have the students bring in copies of the local want ads from newspapers for this activity.

Career Choices gives the students a look at some of the careers that they might pursue in the future. It is also an opportunity for the parents to become involved in career choices for their children.

What Do Your Parents Do? is a parent-participation activity. Parents are invited to the class to present their occupations to the students. They explain what they do and what skills are required to do each particular job. This activity helps some children evaluate their capabilities.

Job Hunting gives students advice on how to write a résumé and tips on appearance and attitude. Even if you teach sixth or seventh graders, the baby-sitting tips or neighborhood job advice will help your students.

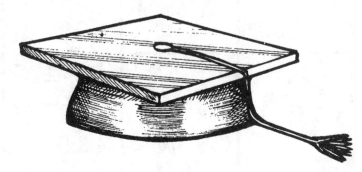

Want Ads

You are ready for your first summer job, or you want to make some extra money by doing part-time work after school. Where do you start? It is easy if your parent owns a business that can employ you. But that is usually not the case, so the best place to look for employment is to check the want ads of the local paper.

Open the classified section of the local newspaper. Look for the job categories in boldfaced print. Make a list of a few job titles that you think you would like to do.

Narrow your list down to the three most interesting and ask yourself these questions:

1. What type of work is described?

2. What skills are required for this job?

3. Do you have these skills? If not, go to another job choice and begin again. If so, continue to question 4.

4. What responsibilities are stated?

5. How much education is required for the job? You may not be educationally ready, and the job might have to wait until you are older.

6. What personal qualifications are needed? Some jobs, such as waitressing, require you to lift heavy trays. Can you do that?

7. How much money will the job pay?

8. Are the job hours convenient for you?

If the job you picked still sounds like something you would like to do, then you should call and explain that you are a student with an interest in the advertised profession. Ask if there is someone willing to answer some questions about the career. Be sure to thank the person you spoke to and write a short thank-you note to follow up. See sample Thank-You Note on page 216.

If you are actually applying for the job, then do not be disappointed if you do not get the first job you interview for. After all, many other students are looking for work, just as you are.

Want Ads *(cont.)*

Just suppose you want to start a local part-time business of your own. A baby-sitting service, a lawn mowing business, a car washing company, or a pet walking business need a different approach. People do not advertise for people to wash their cars. These types of jobs are called service jobs because you are doing a service for other people rather than manufacturing a product to be used.

Service jobs require a different type of advertising. You have to go out to the people and make them aware that you want to provide a service to them. The best technique for this is to advertise door to door. That does not necessarily mean knocking on people's doors; it means creating an ad to place on their doors or in their mailboxes.

Your ad should be eye-catching, neatly written, and checked for spelling mistakes. People will not feel that you can do a good job if your ad is poorly done. Design several ads. Ask your parents for their opinions about the ads and ask them to help correct any mistakes.

In your ads, be sure to include the following information:

    a. the service you are providing

    b. your qualifications

    c. the price you charge for the service

    d. your availability—days and hours you can work

    e. your phone number and your name

When someone answers your ad, be sure to clearly state what your services are and the rate you charge. You cannot change the terms of the agreement after the service is performed.

Create an Ad

Think of a job that you would like to do for your neighbors. Create an ad to place in mailboxes that you think will get you lots of jobs. Remember to be eye-catching and creative!

Practice writing your ad by using the form below. Then you can write your information on a white sheet of 8½" x 11" (21.25 cm x 27.5 cm) paper. When you are satisfied with the results, you can print it onto a colorful sheet of paper or take it to a printer and have copies made.

If you are going to distribute your flyer door to door, take care to fold your flyer neatly. Remember that your flyer reflects you, and people will get the impression that you are sloppy if your flyer is sloppy and crunched up. Following are elements to include.

- Feature the type of work first.
- Introduce yourself.
- Introduce the services you will be providing.
- Explain whether you will provide your own tools or expect to use the employer's.
- Explain that estimates are gladly given.
- Include your name.
- Include your phone number.

Sample Ad:

Lawn Mowing and Yard Clean-Up

If you are looking for a reliable person to mow your lawn and keep your yard clean and free of weeds, then look no further. I will mow your lawn, edge, weed, and water your flower beds weekly or bi-monthly, using your equipment or mine. I also do light hauling and garage clean-up.

Call for free estimates.

Matt White
(543) 231-4512

Your Ad:

Career Choices

Now that you have decided to get a job, how do you decide what to do? The task is not really very difficult, but it does take some self-evaluation and a little extra effort.

The first thing you need to do is make an assessment of your strengths and weaknesses.

My Strengths

1. What can you do well?

   _____

2. What skills can you provide for people?

   _____

3. What do you enjoy doing?

   _____

4. Do you want a full-time job or a part-time job?

   _____

5. What hours or days are you available to work?

   _____

My Weaknesses

1. What things do you not want to do?

   _____

2. What are the things that might prevent you from doing your job?

   _____

3. Do you need your parents' approval or a school's work permit? Is there any reason that you would not get this approval?

   _____

What to Do Next

1. Explore career possibilities in the library and/or guidance office.

2. Read the classified ads in newspapers. Look for some professions that seem interesting to you.

3. Call a professional business organization and ask questions about your possible career choice.

4. Speak to people in the profession and ask them what they do and what the requirements of their jobs are.

Career Choices *(cont.)*

At This Point

If you feel you have found a career you would like to pursue, ask a person in this profession if you may spend a day with him/her at work. This will give you some first-hand knowledge as to what your life's work will entail.

If you are still interested in this profession, then make your plans for your future! Good luck!

Following is a business letter format for you to follow when writing for information about your career.

Your street address
City, State and Zip code
Date

Company name
Street address
City, State and Zip code

Dear Sir/Madam:

Body of your letter

(Be specific and concise about what you desire. Most professionals do not have time to read lengthy letters. Be sure to thank him/her for their time.)

Sincerely,

Your signature
Your typed name

What Do Your Parents Do?

When parents visit your classroom, they are usually taking time from their work day to speak to you. Listen to their presentations carefully. You might find a profession you would like to pursue.

Remember to send a thank-you note to any parents coming to your class. Give your notes to your teacher. All the notes may be mailed together.

Parent Presentation

Name of parent: _____

Parent's occupation: _____

Responsibilities of this profession: _____

_____

_____

_____

_____

_____

_____

What are the daily activities in this job?

_____

_____

_____

_____

_____

_____

What are the educational requirements necessary for this job?

_____

_____

_____

_____

What Do Your Parents Do? *(cont.)*

Parent Presentation

What are the physical requirements for this job?

_____

_____

_____

_____

Is this a job performed by both men and women?

_____

_____

Do you think you would like to do this type of work? Why or why not?

_____

_____

_____

_____

_____

_____

_____

_____

_____

Be sure to be a polite listener and say "Thank you" at the end of the presentation.

Invitation to a Guest Speaker

School address

City, State and Zip code

Date

Dear Sir/Madam:

We are students at Niguel Hills Middle School. We are currently exploring the various careers that we expect to be available to us in the future. As part of our study, we are inviting representatives from many of the local professionals and business people in our area to speak to our class. We would love to hear about your profession, as it might be something we would like to do in the future.

If you are able to find time to speak to us, please contact our teacher, Mrs. Jones at Niguel Hills (714) 555-1122 to make arrangements for your visit.

Sincerely,

Mrs. Jones' Sixth Grade Class

Thank-You Notes

Most guest speakers enjoy reading individual thanks from students. Have each of your students write a thank-you note expressing what they learned from the speaker's visit and what they enjoyed most about the visit. Notes should be informal and signed by the student. Notes can then be placed inside a large manila envelope and mailed to the speaker.

Informal Note

Date_____

Dear_____,

Thank you for speaking to our class on . . .

(Be sure to proofread student's notes for clarity and appropriateness.)

Sincerely,

Student's name

Job Hunting—The Interview

Now that you have decided on the type of job you want and have made an appointment to be interviewed, it is time to learn a few things about how to interview.

Before the Interview

1. **Check Your Wardrobe**

   Look for clothing that is appropriate for the type of job you will be performing. It is not always necessary to wear a dress, a suit, or a tie, but it is usually not proper to wear blue jeans either.

   After you have chosen your outfit, make sure that it is clean and freshly pressed. Check for frayed edges or missing buttons. Future employers often notice these things and feel that this indicates a careless attitude. If you need to purchase a new outfit for your interviews, do so if you can afford it.

2. **Take a Critical Look at Your Appearance**

   Do you need a haircut or a trim? Your hair should be clean and neatly combed and brushed. Examine your nails. Clean under the tips of your nails and trim your cuticles if they need it. Gentlemen, your ragged cuticles and uncut nails are signs of not caring. Ladies, chipped nail polish is a sign of neglect. Your employer might feel that you might be uncaring or neglectful about your responsibilities, too.

Job Hunting—The Interview (cont.)

2. **Take a Critical Look at Your Appearance** (*cont.*)

   Shower or bathe before you go on your interview. Use deodorant. Be careful not to use too much perfume or cologne. Your interviewer might be allergic to scent. It might be a good idea not to use it at all.

   Gentlemen—If you shave, use a new blade to get the closest shave you can.

   Ladies—Pay extra attention to your legs. Nicks and cuts are not becoming. Wear hosiery for that professional look.

3. **Review Your Résumé**

   Your résumé gives your future employer a quick look at your qualifications. Be sure it is up to date. Having outdated information on a résumé can spoil your chance of being hired.

Day of the Interview

1. Just before you are ready to leave the house, check your appearance. This extra check will give you confidence about your over-all look.

2. Check the directions to the place where your interview will be held. Getting lost can ruin your job chances.

3. Plan to arrive at your interview at least 15 minutes early. Bring a book or a news magazine with you to read while you are waiting. Do not bring any type of reading material that might offend someone.

4. Wait patiently for the interviewer. Sometimes interviewers can get delayed and be running behind.

Job Hunting—The Interview

During the Interview

1. First impressions mean a lot. The immediate look your interviewer gets might make the difference between getting a job or not.

2. Smile, introduce yourself, and shake the interviewer's hand with a firm, strong handshake. Even if you are a female, a confident handshake reveals a confident person.

3. Try to be relaxed and listen carefully to what the interviewer says and asks.

4. Do not fidget in your seat. Sit straight and keep your feet and hands still. The interviewer knows you are nervous, and you know you are nervous, so do not make it worse by squirming.

5. Answer the interviewer's questions honestly. If you cannot do something, do not say you can just to get the job. You may get the job, but you may be fired quickly.

After the Interview

1. Thank the interviewer for his/her time and for interviewing you.

2. Leave the interviewing room; do not dawdle. Do not ask any additional questions. The time for questions was before the end of the interview.

3. It is always hard to wait, but everyone has to go through this. In a few days you can call and inquire as to the status of the job you interviewed for. If it has been filled, thank the person on the phone and continue your job search.

4. It is not uncommon to fail to get the first job you apply for. This does not mean that there is something wrong with you. There may have been many people applying for a single available position.

NOTE: Many employers keep copies of résumés on file in case another position becomes available.

Interview Questions

Most employers usually ask the same types of questions. Choose another student in class and practice asking and answering the questions below. Add some questions you think your future employer might ask, and you will be ready for your interview.

Questions the Interviewer Might Ask

1. Why do you want this particular job?

2. What are your qualifications?

3. What particular skills do you have that will make you an asset to this company?

4. What is your educational background?

5. What is your past work experience?

6. Why did you choose this company?

7. What are your future plans?

8. Are you planning to go to college?

9. Where would you like to be (that is, in your career) in five years?

10. Knowing what you know about our company, do you think this is something you would like to do after you are out of school?

11. Why do you think you are more qualified for this job than the other applicants?

12. Do you have any special skills that you can bring to this job?

Questions You Might Ask the Interviewer

1. What would the job entail?

2. What would my responsibilities be?

3. What hours would I be required to work?

4. What physical tasks, if any, would I be required to do?

5. Would your company be understanding about my school schedule? (midterms, finals, band, sports, etc.)

6. What are your other employees like? (male/female, ages, etc.)

7. May I tour your facilities?

Writing a Résumé

When applying for a job, it is always a feather in your cap if you have prepared a résumé for your employer. A résumé is a biographical sketch of you. It includes personal information as well as any work history and educational background. Résumés change as your work history and personal situation change. Résumés should be updated every few years or when your personal history changes.

There are many ways of writing a résumé. On the next two pages you will find an outline followed by a sample résumé of one of those ways. After reading those, prepare a résumé about yourself in the space below. Continue on the back of this page if needed.

Résumé Outline

Name

Work Address   **Home Address**

Street Address   Street Address
City, State, Zip   City, State, Zip
Phone   Phone

Objective   State your objective here.

Education   Begin with the most recent schooling

Experience   What qualifications do you have?

Honors   Honors in school

Activities   Activities that you engage in (in or out of school).

Section Heading   This can be any information relevant to your résumé.

References   Two seems to be the standard number for references. Include full name, address, and phone number.

Sample Résumé

Résumé
of
Samantha Smith

Work Address
McDonald's
2121 Burger Way
Anytown, New York 11573
Phone: (543) 321-1234

Home Address
26-76 Fourth Street
Anytown, New York 11573
Phone: (543) 321-9807

Objective	To obtain a full time position as a secretary.
Education	(1993–present) Newton Secretarial School Anytown, New York
Experience	(1993–present) Various positions at McDonald's • Counter Service • Customer Service • Personnel Office
Honors	• Newton Secretarial School • Number 1 in class • Shorthand Student of the Year • Voted Most Likely to Succeed
Activities	• Sports: tennis, golf • Reading—interested in mysteries
Section Heading	• Very Organized • Intelligent • Responsible
References	Mr. Ronald McDonald McDonald's 2121 Burger Way Anytown, New York 11573 Mrs. June Trance Newton Secretarial School 3456 Seaside Way Anytown, New York 11573

Why School ?

The activities in this section enable the students to gain an understanding of the value of a formal education and the importance of completing their formal education.

School Report Card provides the students an opportunity to evaluate their school and gives the teacher some insights into the student's perceptions about their school. Knowing the outcome of this informal survey allows the teacher to better provide for the students.

Aw Mom, Do I Hafta Go to School? is a phrase everyone has heard before, but what is the real reason children do not want to go to school? In this activity the students are given an opportunity to evaluate their school. Questions cover both the academic and elective programs, along with the environment of the school.

The Ideal School is a creative group project. The students are asked to create the perfect school—a delightful, thought-provoking project for all.

My School's Report Card

Now is your chance to grade your school. In this activity sheet you will be evaluating your school and giving it a grade. In following activities you will be asked to make suggestions for improving your school environment.

Answer the following questions about your school. Be sure to explain your answers.

1. I enjoy going to school because . . .

   _____

   _____

2. School is a place where . . .

   _____

   _____

3. The teachers in my school . . .

   _____

   _____

4. When I have a problem, I can (always) (sometimes) (never) find someone to talk to. Underline one of the above options and explain your reasons for choosing it.

   _____

   _____

5. My school is a place that I (can) (cannot) feel proud of. Underline one of the above options and explain your reasons for choosing it.

   _____

   _____

6. My teachers have (always) (sometimes) (never) encouraged me to do my best. Underline one of the above options and explain your reasons for choosing it.

   _____

   _____

7. School (is) (is not) a safe place for the students. Underline one of the above options and explain your reasons for choosing it.

   _____

   _____

8. Teachers (always) (usually) (sometimes) (never) provide a stimulating and challenging academic program. Underline one of the above options and explain your reasons for choosing it.

   _____

   _____

9. My school needs many improvements. They are . . .

   _____

   _____

10. If I could improve my school, I would . . .

    _____

    _____

The grade that I give my school is _____ .

Aw, Mom, Do I Hafta Go to School?

At one time or another everyone has said those words, but we do not have to feel that way if we are given an opportunity to make suggestions about our school.

In this activity you will discuss whether you should be required to go to school. Be factual in answering these questions. Unsupported opinions will not be valid. Be honest in your answers.

Working in groups of five, answer the following:

1. Why should students be required to attend school through high school?

   _____

   _____

   _____

   _____

2. Why do parents think it is important for children to attend school through high school? (Ask them this evening.)

   _____

   _____

   _____

   _____

3. Speak to businesses in the community and ask them this question: Why should children stay in school?

   _____

   _____

   _____

   _____

4. What are the advantages of staying in school?

   _____

   _____

   _____

   _____

Aw, Mom, Do I Hafta Go to School? *(cont.)*

5. What are the disadvantages of staying in school?

_____

_____

_____

6. Why do students drop out?

_____

_____

_____

7. At what grade level do they most frequently drop out?   (Call your school district's main office; they have records of this information.)

_____

_____

_____

8. What are some solutions to keeping students in school?

_____

_____

_____

9. Where or to whom do students go when they need help?

_____

_____

_____

10. What other programs or personnel are available to help these students?

_____

_____

_____

11. Identify some strengths and weaknesses that your school's programs have.

_____

_____

_____

Present your finding to your class.

The Ideal School

Working in design groups, create the school of the future. In this school everything is perfect. Students want to be there. Teachers and administration are supportive. Parents, teachers, and students work together to make this school a place where students drop IN—not OUT.

Brainstorm the requirements that you want your school to have. List those requirements below. (Don't forget a name for your school.)

The Ideal School *(cont.)*

Plan a design for your school. Include classrooms, offices, lunch area, library, gym, etc. Think of any areas that you would like in your school. Don't forget the rest rooms!

Use the area below for some of your ideas.

When you feel that you have a plan for the ideal school, ask your teacher for a sheet of butcher paper and draw a floor plan for your school.

The Ideal School *(cont.)*

Write a description of the educational programs your ideal school has and how the students attending your school will benefit from them.

The Ideal School *(cont.)*

Write the description of the nonacademic programs your ideal school has. Examples: sports, drama, music, etc.

Present your school to the "community" (your classmates) and vote on the designs that are best.

School and Career Choice

It always helps to have hard facts in advance to help us make our choices. Preparing for a career often depends on choices made about our schooling, and we need to know just what kind of life we are preparing for. Answers to the following questions may well help you make your own choices about school and career.

- What does it pay?
- What does it cost?
- How much do you need to earn to own it?

This activity will give you an idea of what you will need to earn to afford all of life's little necessities and luxuries.

Find the average earning per year for the following careers:

(If you can find only a weekly or monthly wage, calculate the yearly pay by multiplying the monthly wage by 12 months or the weekly wage by 52 weeks.)

- Sanitation Worker _____
- Store Clerk _____
- Salesman/Saleswoman _____
- Accountant _____
- Teacher _____
- Lawyer _____
- Doctor _____
- Engineer _____
- Mechanic_____
- The profession you want to follow_____

Find the cost of feeding the average family of four for one week. (You must first plan what to feed your family.)

List five things you would like to own and find out the cost of each. (car, VCR, TV, etc.)

-
-
-
-
-

Add any other items that you would need as a self-supporting adult.

Calculate the total cost for all your needs.

Can you afford all this?

Multicultural Projects for the Year

Many middle schools today are attended by students with varied ethnic backgrounds. As teachers meet the academic needs of their students, so must they meet the diverse cultural needs of the students. The following activities are just a sampling of exercises that are designed to make students aware of others' cultures.

Each section is divided into quarter activities to correspond to the previous sections of this book.

First Quarter

- Ramadan Fast and Id-Ui-Fitr
- Tet-Trung-Thu
- Mexican Independence Day
- American Indian Day
- Rosh Hashanah and Yom Kippur
- Oktoberfest

Second Quarter

- El Dia de los Muertos
- Diwali
- Loy Krathong

Third Quarter

- Mardi Gras

Fourth Quarter

- Arbor Day/Earth Day
- Urini Nal

The Ramadan Fast and Id-Ui-Fitr

Ramadan is a sacred Moslem observance. People in Jordan, Morocco, Syria, and other Moslem countries celebrate this holiday. In late summer or early fall when the full moon appears, the Ramadan fast begins. Moslem people will not eat, drink, or smoke from sunrise to sunset. They spend their days praying and remembering their prophet Mohammed. The Moslems have been celebrating this holiday for more than 1300 years!

The fasting and praying continue until the next full moon appears. As this day approaches, the people stand on the rooftops searching the sky until they see the moon. At the first sighting, there are shouts of joy and the beating of drums. This event signals the start of the three day-festival known as Id-Ui-Fitr. Id means "happiness" and Fitr means "breaking the fast." As you can see, this is a celebration that the month-long fast is over.

Learn more about this Moslem holiday by answering these questions.

Use your encyclopedias for help in this research.

1. What is the name given to a Moslem temple?

   _____

2. What is the Koran?

   _____

   _____

   _____

3. The Moslems enjoy a dish called *saiwiyan*. Find out just what is in this delicious dish.

   _____

   _____

   _____

   _____

   _____

   _____

4. Draw a map of the Moslem countries. (See page 235.)

5. Draw the flags of the Moslem countries. (See page 236.)

Map of Moslem Countries

Draw and color the Moslem countries. Write the name of each country on the map.

Flags of Moslem Countries

Jordan	Pakistan
Morocco	**Syria**

Other Moslem Countries

Find and draw the flags for as many other countries as you can that celebrate the Ramadan fast.

Tet-Trung-Thu

Legend states that the Tet-Trung-Thu festival began long, long ago. It is a holiday based on the lunar calendar. The exact day of the celebration is unknown, but Tet-Trung-Thu is celebrated around the fifteenth of September, which is the eighth lunar month. The people of Vietnam tell two stories about how this festival came to be. One story is that the Emperor Minh-Mang fell asleep in his garden. There he dreamed that he met a beautiful queen and danced a beautiful dance with her in the moonlight. The Emperor was so saddened when he awoke that he asked his servants to perform the moon dance he taught them and to bake the moon cakes he shared with the princess.

The second version is one that is not uncommon for cultures which follow the lunar cycle. The Vietnam people believe that the moon is at its fullest and most beautiful during the eighth month.

Almost all the Tet-Trung-Thu festival is for children. On festival night, children swing colorful lanterns, dance, eat little moon cakes, and listen to legends about Hang Nga, the moon fairy.

Today, children of Vietnamese ancestry eat moon cakes that are sometimes filled with black beans mashed with sugar. Moon cakes are round and can also be filled with pork, watermelon seeds, or shark fins.

Outside Vietnam, Tet Trung Thu is a time for the Vietnamese people to make their children happy with a day that will be remembered all year long. It is a time to preserve and pass on their culture and their language. It is a time to remember their roots. Recent festivals in Southern California have drawn thousands of people to celebrate Tet-Trung-Thu with traditional Vietnamese food, performances by dancers and martial arts groups, music, and singing. And just as they would in Vietnam, the children listen to stories about Hang Nga while munching on moon cakes.

Tet-Trung-Thu (cont.)

Make your own lantern for Tet-Trung-Thu.

1. Choose a colorful piece of construction paper.

2. Fold the paper lengthwise.

3. Draw a line one inch (2.5 cm) from the edge and carefully cut evenly spaced slits to the line.

4. Open the paper and fold into a circle, overlapping the uncut edges.

5. Staple or tape at the overlapping spots.

6. Gently push down on the circle to spread the middle of the paper. Glue tissue paper pieces on the bottom edge.

7. Attach a string to the top and hang your lantern in your room for Tet-Trung-Thu.

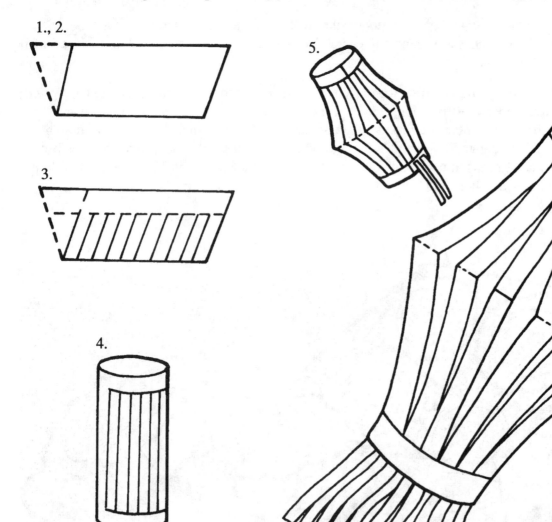

1., 2.

3.

4.

5.

6.

238

Mexican Independence Day

Viva la independencia! Viva Mexico! are the words spoken all over Mexico on Independence Day. Every year since September 16, 1810, bells ring out and shouts are heard throughout the streets of Mexico.

Mexican Independence Day is the remembrance of Mexico's fight to win its freedom from Spain. On that day long ago, the Catholic priest Miguel Hidalgo rang the bells that signaled Mexican Independence in the town of Dolores, Mexico. It began an 11-year war of rebellion against Spain. Father Hidalgo was captured by the Spanish in 1811 and shot as a traitor.

Today the President of Mexico rings the bells in honor of Father Hidalgo and independence! People gather in the town plazas all over the country to hear their mayors give the *Grito de Dolores* (Cry of Dolores). The streets are decorated with flags and wreaths of flowers. Bands play, bells ring, fireworks explode, and everyone cries out, "Viva Mexico!" Boys carry little toy *toritos*, or bulls, over their shoulders as they dash through the street. On the tails of the bulls are placed firecrackers, and the sparks fly everywhere as the boys run.

The biggest event of this celebration is the National Lottery. The tickets are inexpensive, and almost everyone in Mexico buys a ticket. The winning ticket is drawn in Mexico City and announced over television and radio. Imagine the excitement of the people!

Mexican Independence "Torito"

Make a papier mâché bull for Mexican Independence Day.

1. Cut newspaper into long strips.

2. Blow up two balloons and glue them together to form the head and body of the bull.

3. In a bowl pour some liquid starch. Dip the strips of newspaper into the starch. Thoroughly wet the newspaper and run it through two of your fingers to wring out the excess.

4. Continue wrapping the wet starched strips around the balloons until you have shaped the head and body of the bull.

5. Mold a strip of paper for the tail and the ears and attach carefully to the body and head.

6. Set aside the bull to dry overnight.

7. When your bull has dried, you can paint and decorate it as you wish.

Now you are ready for Mexican Independence Day!

American Indian Day

In 1914, Red Fox James campaigned for a national holiday to honor the American Indian people. The first to observe this day were the Boy Scouts in New York State. Red Fox James traveled more than 4,000 miles across the United States to win recognition for the American Indian.

Many of the famous Indians you read about in history are remembered during American Indian Day. Learn more about them. Research one of these names and prepare a short report to give your classmates about their importance in Native American history.

Cochise	**Tecumseh**
Geronimo	**Massasoit**
Chief Joseph	**Pvt. Ira Hayes**
Squanto	**King Phillip**
Sitting Bull	**Pontiac**
Osceola	**Black Hawk**
Jim Thorpe	**Montezuma**
Deganawidah	**Powhatan**
Joseph Brant	**Manuelito**
Sacajawea	**Cuauhtemoc**
Sequoyah	

Rosh Hashanah and Yom Kippur

To Jewish families today, Rosh Hashanah and Yom Kippur are the holiest of days, but it was not always this way. Long, long ago the gathering of the harvest meant the ending of one year and the beginning of the new year. So Rosh Hashanah and Yom Kippur began much like other holidays which began as harvest celebrations. These days are celebrated as they were centuries ago in the middle of September or October.

The celebration of Rosh Hashanah through Yom Kippur is now a sacred and holy holiday spanning the first 10 days of the Jewish month of Tisri, known together as The High Holy Days. Jews around the world welcome the new year with thoughts of all the wrongdoings of the past year. The holiday begins with Rosh Hashanah, a celebration welcoming in the New Year. Families join together for a special holiday meal. A favorite food during this meal is halvah, a kind of bread that is dipped in honey.

The 10-day celebration ends with the solemn observance of Yom Kippur, The Day of Atonement. During this time the Jews believe that their names are written in The Book of Life with a listing of their good and bad deeds. From sundown to sundown, Jews fast to cleanse their bodies and to symbolize the cleansing of the soul.

At sundown on Yom Kippur, the holy days end with the blowing of the shofar or ram's horn.

Activity

✡ Write a letter to the Rabbi at your local synagogue. Invite him to speak to your class about Rosh Hashanah and Yom Kippur. Place your rough draft in the space below.

Oktoberfest

Oktoberfest is a festival celebrated by the German people. It is a colorful outdoor celebration that begins in September and lasts 16 days. Oktoberfest always ends on the first Sunday in October. Today many people in the United States celebrate at various gatherings throughout the month of October.

Oktoberfest dates back to 1810, when the King of Bavaria presented his kingdom with this celebration in honor of his son's marriage. Each year after this first celebration, Oktoberfest continued to be celebrated with even more flourish. Events and games were added and the festival became even more grand.

During Oktoberfest men, women, and children dress in the costumes of their ancestors. There is a parade of marching bands and white, horse-drawn wagons from Bavarian breweries.

A large variety of food is consumed during Oktoberfest. Vendors set tables laden with beef, knockwurst, buns, cabbage, pastries, and sweets. All the celebrants have their fill at the Oktoberfest celebration.

The highlight of the Oktoberfest is the songs, singing, and dancing that take place in the traditional costumes.

Oktoberfest *(cont.)*

During the Oktoberfest celebration the men and women dress in traditional costumes. Investigate the traditional dress worn by both men and women and read the directions below.

Men

Draw a gentleman of Bavaria in his traditional dress. Men and boys wear short leather breeches called *lederhosen* , fancy embroidered suspenders, woolen knee socks, and pointed Tyrolean hats.

Woman

Draw a girl of Bavaria in her traditional dress. The women and girls wear flowered dirndl skirts with several layers of petticoats, and white peasant blouses with lace bodices or vests.

Bavarian Man	Bavarian Woman

El Dia de los Muertos

Around the time those of us in the United States celebrate Halloween, our neighbors to the south celebrate El Dia de los Muertos, or The Day of the Dead. This is the day when the dead return to their homes and visit their families! El Dia de los Muertos, like Halloween, is a fun holiday.

Bakeries and toy stores start preparing sweet breads shaped like skulls, ghosts, and bones. This is called *pan de los muertos,* or bread of the dead.

Families also prepare for this celebration by setting out photos of their relatives who have died. They set out food for the returning ghosts, and the family carries meals to the cemetery where loved ones are buried. They decorate grave sites with yellow and orange flowers and burn incense as they pray.

In the United States, El Dia de los Muertos is celebrated with fireworks, cultural displays, art shows, and street fairs.

One of the favorite activities of El Dia de los Muertos is to create eerie pictures. You can do this too! Cut a small size potato in half. Draw a ghost, skull, or scary design on one half. Carefully carve out your design. Dip the potato into black paint and create your Day of the Dead design. Decorate the space below with your personal creation.

Diwali

In late October or early November you will see thousands of twinkling little lights shining over the country of India. This announces the *Diwali* (sometimes spelled Divali) holiday. Diwali is not one, but four, separate holidays that are celebrated one right after the other. There is really no connection between the holidays except for the time of year that they are celebrated.

The first of these holidays is *Dhana trayodashi.*   This one-day celebration is marked by businesses settling their accounts with their customers and offering prayers to *Lakshimi,* the Hindu goddess of prosperity and fortune. The Hindus believe that these offerings will ensure a prosperous business year.

The second celebration is to honor the moon. The Hindus believe that the moon changes faces every 14 days, and so they serve 14 different dishes at their festival dinner.

Yama is the third celebration. This is a special family holiday where brothers and sisters make promises of love and loyalty to each other. If there are no brothers or sisters, then a cousin fills in. The children spend the day together and share a special evening meal. This is probably a celebration we might wish to share in America or all over the world.

Lastly is *Bali Worship Day.* This day commemorates the battle between the legendary character Vishnu and the monster, Naraka Chaturdashi. As the legend goes, Naraka Chaturdashi captured 16,000 beautiful maidens, and it was Vishnu who did battle with him for their release. The holiday celebrates the winning of good over evil.

During Diwali, Indian homes are scrubbed clean and anointed with oils and flowers. Women create elaborate pictures called *alpanas* on their living room floors. Schools are closed the day before the holiday so children can make *dipas.* Dipas are oil-burning lamps that light balconies, pathways, rooftops, and gardens.

Alpana   Lakshimi

Diwali *(cont.)*

Create your own *dipa* in celebration of Diwali.

Materials

- ¼ lb. (110 grams) self-hardening clay for each student
- acrylic paints in assorted colors
- candle wick—about 3" (8 cm) long
- mustard oil

Procedure

1. Roll the clay into a ball and flatten with the palm of your hand.

2. Shape the sides up so that they form a saucer-shaped container.

3. Press the wick firmly into the center of the saucer and allow to dry.

4. Paint the outer area of the saucer in beautiful, colorful designs.

5. When your saucer is dry, place about ½" (1.3 cm) of mustard oil in the bottom and light the wick. *Care should be taken not to put your dipa in an area that could start a fire!* Check with your parent for permission before you light it!

Loy Krathong

In November in the country of Thailand there is a holiday that has been a favorite of children for more than 600 years. It is the holiday of *Loy Krathong*. During this holiday the people of Thailand ask forgiveness of the goddess of water for having dirtied the rivers all year long.

Loy means "to float" and *Krathong* means "leaf," so it is the tradition in Thailand for children to construct tiny boats out of banana leaves. Candles, coins, or incense sticks are placed in the candles and floated down the river. Legend says that if the light from the candle lasts until the krathong disappears down the river, then the child's wish shall be granted.

Loy Krathong is certainly a very joyous holiday in Thailand.

Create your own krathong.

What to Do

Cut a banana leaf and shape it into a boat shape. Fasten the edges together with bamboo skewers. Float your krathong in a basin of water or a wading pool. Then take the krathong challenge if you dare!

The Krathong Challenge

After all the boats have been constructed, hold a friendly regatta. To win, your boat will have to be the strongest and last the longest. Follow the steps to see if you are a winner!

1. Measure the length and width of your boat. _____

2. Measure the height of your boat._____

3. What is the volume of your boat? _____

4. Predict how many pennies your boat will hold without sinking. _____

5. Count your pennies as you place them one at a time into your boat. The boat that holds the most pennies without sinking wins. How many pennies did your boat hold before it sank? _____

Mardi Gras

Mardi Gras takes place each February or March on Shrove Tuesday. Shrove Tuesday is the day before Lent. Lent is the forty-day period preceding Easter. During Mardi Gras, people attend magnificent balls, parties, and parades. It is the loud and lively time before the serious and solemn Lenten period.

Mardi Gras is celebrated in many countries, as well as the United States. Perhaps you have attended or read about the Mardi Gras parade held in New Orleans each year. It is the most famous of all the Mardi Gras celebrations. The first Mardi Gras parade in Louisiana was held in 1704 by the French settlers. Today everyone in New Orleans takes part in this celebration, and each year people travel far and wide to be in New Orleans at Mardi Gras! During the parades everyone celebrates by wearing ornate masks and dressing in costumes representing clowns, monsters, and animals. There are beautiful floats, and fun is had by all.

Activities

1. The countries of France, Spain, Portugal, Norway, Denmark, and England all celebrate Mardi Gras. Find out how each country celebrates Mardi Gras in its own special way and write your findings below and on the back of this page.

2. Investigate the history of the Mardi Gras on the island of Saint Thomas in the Virgin Islands and compare it to the other celebrations you have learned about.

3. Create your own Mardi Gras mask and display it in your room. Remember that most masks worn at Mardi Gras are outrageous!

Mardi Gras Mask

Arbor Day

Arbor Day is celebrated in the United States during the month of April. This holiday encourages everyone to care for and conserve the trees in the forests.

Arbor Day began with a man named J. Sterling Morton in 1872. Mr. Morton believed that the state of Nebraska did not have enough trees, so he suggested to the state agricultural board that they have an annual tree-planting day and award prizes to the county that planted the most trees. During that first Arbor Day, Nebraskans planted over one million trees. Today Arbor Day is more than just a Nebraskan holiday. It is celebrated around the world in such countries as Israel, Canada, Norway, and even South Africa.

Some countries and states celebrate Arbor Day at different times of the year because of weather and climate conditions. Do your part in this Arbor Day celebration and ask permission from your principal for your class to plant a tree in honor of Arbor Day. If the permission is granted, contact a local nursery and ask if they will donate a tree.

In many areas of the United States, the Arbor Day celebration is held in conjunction with Earth Day. Investigate the history of Earth Day and prepare a report to your class. Plan some Earth Day posters that can be displayed around your school and community to remind everyone to conserve and protect our planet.

Some classes may wish to schedule a visit to an arboretum, an outdoor laboratory where trees and other woody plants are grown in natural conditions. It is an ideal way to view a wide variety of trees from many different parts of the world. The trees are often grouped by family and species, helping us to recognize scientific classifications. Arboretums are generally open to the public, and they welcome visitors, hoping to encourage interest and appreciation for the earth's botanical wonders. Arbor Lodge, the former home of J. Sterling Morton in Nebraska City, Nebraska, is a type of arboretum featuring 250 distinct varieties of trees and shrubs.

Urini Nal

If you are Korean, then you know that Urini Nal is a celebration honoring the children. In 1919, Chung Hwan Bang felt that the children of Korea should be honored for the respect and obedience that they gave parents and elders throughout the year.

On May 5th, schools close, and parents plan special activities for their children. The Children's Park and many theaters are free for the children on Urini Nal. Many businesses give the children free treats in honor of their day. Boys and girls spend the day painting pictures, creating stories, poems, and attending various puppet shows. There are many contests for the children, and prizes are awarded to the best in each event. Some of the favorite foods are rice cakes, barbecued meats, and popcorn.

Celebrate the festival of the children, Urini Nal, by writing a puppet show with your classmates and creating the puppets to perform it. Then invite some other classes to your puppet show and popcorn festival in honor of Urini Nal.

252

Glossary

Reproduce the following glossary for your class or assign five to ten words weekly for your students to define.

A

Academic

Of, relating to, or characteristic of a school, especially one of higher learning.

Achievement

1. The act of accomplishing or finishing.

2. Something accomplished successfully, especially by means of exertion, skill, practice, or perseverance.

Acquaintance

Knowledge of a person acquired by a relationship less intimate than friendship.

Acquire

To get by one's own efforts.

Activity

An educational process or procedure intended to stimulate learning through actual experience.

Administration

Management of an institution, public or private.

Adolescence

The period of physical and psychological development from the onset of puberty to maturity.

Advertisement

A notice, such as a poster, newspaper display, or paid announcement in the electronic media, designed to attract public attention or patronage.

Alcohol

Intoxicating liquor.

Alcoholic

A person who drinks alcoholic substances habitually and to excess or who suffers from alcoholism.

Algebra

A generalization of arithmetic in which symbols, usually letters of the alphabet, represent numbers or members of a specified set of numbers and are related by operations that hold for all numbers in the set.

B

Behavior

The actions or reactions of persons or things in response to external or internal stimuli.

Benefit

Something that promotes or enhances well-being.

Body Language

The bodily gestures, postures, and facial expressions by which a person communicates nonverbally with others.

Glossary *(cont.)*

Brainstorm
To consider or investigate (an issue, for example) by engaging in shared problem solving.

Business
The occupation, work, or trade in which a person is engaged.

C

Campus
The grounds of a school, college, university, or hospital.

Career
A chosen pursuit; a profession or occupation.

Cartoon
A drawing depicting a humorous situation, often accompanied by a caption.

CD/ROM
A compact disk that functions as a read-only memory.

Chamber of Commerce
An association of business persons and merchants for the promotion of commercial interests in the community.

Characteristic
A feature that helps to distinguish a person or thing; distinctive.

Choice
The act of choosing; selection.

Class
1. A group of students or alumni who have the same year of graduation.
2. A group of students who meet at a regularly scheduled time to study the same subject.

Classroom
A room or place especially in a school in which classes are conducted.

Coat of Arms
Heraldry.
1. A tabard or surcoat blazoned with bearings.
2. An arrangement of bearings, usually depicted on and around a shield, that indicates ancestry and distinctions; a representation of bearings.

College
An institution of higher learning that grants the bachelor's degree in liberal arts or science or both.

Comic Strip
A narrative running cartoon.

Compliment
An expression of praise, admiration, or congratulation.

Compromise
1. A settlement of differences in which each side makes concessions.
2. The result of such a settlement.

Glossary *(cont.)*

Conflict

A state of disharmony between incompatible or antithetical persons, ideas, or interests; a clash.

Conscience

1. The awareness of a moral or ethical aspect to one's conduct together with the urge to prefer right over wrong.

2. A source of moral or ethical judgment or pronouncement.

3. Conformity to one's own sense of right conduct.

Controlled Substance

A drug or chemical substance whose possession and use are regulated under the Controlled Substances Act.

Cooperate

To work or act together toward a common end or purpose.

Counselor

A person who gives counsel; an adviser.

Creative

Having to do with the mind's imagination.

Custodian

A janitor.

D

Data

Factual information, especially information organized for analysis or used to reason or make decisions.

Decision

1. The passing of judgment on an issue under consideration.
2. The act of reaching a conclusion or making up one's mind.
3. A conclusion or judgment reached or pronounced; a verdict.

Define

To state the precise meaning of (a word or sense of a word, for example).

Descendant

1. Moving downward; descending.
2. Proceeding by descent from an ancestor; offspring or child.

Design

To create or execute in an artistic or highly skilled manner.

Devise

To form, plan, or arrange in the mind; design or contrive.

Diagram

A plan, sketch, drawing, or outline designed to demonstrate or explain how something works or to clarify the relationship between the parts of a whole.

Discipline

Training expected to produce a specific character or pattern of behavior, especially training that produces moral or mental improvement.

Glossary *(cont.)*

Display

To present or hold up to view.

Drug

A chemical substance, such as a narcotic or hallucinogen, that affects the central nervous system, causing changes in behavior and often addiction.

Drunk

Intoxicated with alcoholic liquor to the point of impairment of physical and mental faculties.

E

Education

The knowledge or skill obtained or developed by a learning process. A program of instruction of a specified kind or level.

Emotion

An intense mental state that arises subjectively rather than through conscious effort and is often accompanied by physiological changes; a strong feeling.

Employ

1. To engage the services of; put to work; to provide with gainful work.

2. To put to use or service.

Employee

A person who works for another in return for financial or other compensation.

Employment

The act of employing; the state of being employed.

Encounter

A meeting, especially one that is unplanned, unexpected, or brief.

Encourage

To inspire with hope, courage, or confidence; hearten.

Environment

1. The combination of external physical conditions that affect and influence the growth, development, and survival of organisms.

2. The complex of social and cultural conditions affecting the nature of an individual or a community.

Equal

Having the same privileges, status, or rights.

Expectation

Prospects, especially of success or gain.

Experience

Active participation in events or activities, leading to the accumulation of knowledge or skill.

Expression

1. The manner in which one expresses oneself, especially in speaking, depicting, or performing.

2. A facial aspect or a look that conveys a special feeling.

Glossary *(cont.)*

F

Faculty

1. A body of teachers.
2. All the members of a learned profession.

Family

1. A fundamental social group in society typically consisting of a man and woman and their offspring; two or more people who share goals and values, have long-term commitments to one another, and reside usually in the same dwelling place.
2. All the members of a household under one roof.
3. A group of persons sharing common ancestry.
4. Lineage, especially distinguished lineage.

Family Tree

A genealogical diagram of a family's ancestry.

Fear

1. A feeling of agitation and anxiety caused by the presence or imminence of danger; a state or condition marked by this feeling.
2. A feeling of disquiet or apprehension.

Folder

A flexible cover folded in the center and used as a holder for loose paper.

Follower

One that imitates or copies another.

Formal

1. Following or being in accord with accepted forms, conventions, or regulations.
2. Executed, carried out, or done in proper or regular form.

Friend

A person whom one knows, likes, and trusts.

G

Group

A number of individuals or things considered together because of similarities.

H

Habit

An addiction, especially to a narcotic drug.

Habit-forming

Capable of leading to physiological or psychological dependence.

Handicapped

Physically or mentally disabled.

Glossary (cont.)

Handshake
The grasping of hands by two people, as in greeting or leave-taking.

Health
1. Soundness, especially of body or mind; freedom from disease or abnormality.
2. A condition of optimal well-being.

Hero
In mythology and legend, a man, often of divine ancestry, who is endowed with great courage and strength, celebrated for his bold exploits, and favored by the gods.

Heroine
1. A woman noted for courage and daring action.
2. A woman noted for special achievement in a particular field.
3. The principal female character in a novel, poem, or dramatic presentation.

Honest
Marked by or displaying integrity; upright.

I

Idiom
Regional speech or dialect.

Impression
An effect, a feeling, or an image retained as a consequence of experience.

Individual
By or for one person.
Existing as a distinct entity; separate.

Initiative
The power or ability to begin or to follow through energetically with a plan or task; enterprise and determination.

Insecure
Not sure or certain; doubtful.

Integrity
Steadfast adherence to a strict moral or ethical code.

J

Jeopardize
Expose to loss or injury; imperil.

Job
1. A regular activity performed in exchange for payment, especially as one's trade, occupation, or profession.
2. A position in which one is employed.

Glossary *(cont.)*

Judge

Form an opinion or estimation of after careful consideration.

Junior High School

A school in the U.S. system generally including the seventh, eighth, and sometimes ninth grades.

K

Knowledge

Familiarity, awareness, or understanding gained through experience or study.

L

Learning

Knowledge or skill gained through schooling or study.

Legal

Concerned with law.

Library

A place in which literary and artistic materials, such as books, periodicals, newspapers, pamphlets, prints, records, and tapes, are kept for reading, reference, or lending.

Life

1. A living being, especially a person.
2. The physical, mental, and spiritual experiences that constitute existence.

LSD

A crystalline compound derived from lysergic acid and used as a powerful hallucinogenic drug. Also called acid, lysergic acid diethylamide.

M

Magazine

A periodical containing a collection of articles, stories, pictures, or other features.

Majority

The amount by which the greater number of votes cast, as in an election, exceeds the total number of remaining votes.

Member

One who belongs to a group or an organization.

Middle School

A school at a level between elementary and high school, typically including grades five through eight.

Motivate

To provide with an incentive; move to action; impel.

N

Glossary *(cont.)*

Narcotic

An addictive drug, such as opium, that reduces pain, alters mood and behavior, and usually induces sleep or stupor. Natural and synthetic narcotics are used in medicine to control pain.

Neglect

To fail to care for or attend to properly.

Neighborhood

The people who live near one another or in a particular district or area.

Nicotine

A colorless, poisonous alkaloid derived from the tobacco plant and used as an insecticide. It is the substance in tobacco to which smokers can become addicted.

O

Observation

The act of noting and recording something, such as a phenomenon, with instruments.

Obtain

To succeed in gaining possession of as the result of planning or endeavor; acquire.

Occupation

An activity that serves as one's regular source of livelihood; a vocation.

Office

A place in which business, clerical, or professional activities are conducted.

Organize

To put together into an orderly, functional, structured whole.

Over-the-Counter (O.T.C.)

Medication or drugs which can be sold legally without a doctor's prescription.

P

Participation

The act of taking part or sharing in something.

Part-Time

For or during less than the customary or standard time.

Perception

Insight, intuition, or knowledge.

Personal

Relating to a particular person; private.

Personnel

The body of persons employed by or active in an organization, business, or service.

Pharmacy

1. The art of preparing and dispensing drugs.

2. A place where drugs are sold; a drugstore. In this sense, also called *apothecary*.

Plagiarize

To use and pass off as one's own (the ideas or writings of another).

Glossary *(cont.)*

Popularity

The quality or state of being popular, especially the state of being widely admired, accepted, or sought after.

Potential

Having possibility, capability, or power.

Prejudice

An adverse judgment or opinion formed beforehand or without knowledge or examination of the facts.

Prescription

1. A written order, especially by a physician, for the preparation and administration of a medicine or other treatment.

2. A prescribed medicine or other treatment.

Pride

A sense of one's own proper dignity or value; self-respect.

Profession

An occupation requiring considerable training and specialized study.

Professional

Engaging in a given activity as a source of livelihood or as a career.

Prohibit

To forbid by authority. To prevent.

Proper

1. Characterized by appropriateness or suitability; fitting.

2. Called for by rules or conventions; correct.

Proud

Feeling pleasurable satisfaction over an act, a possession, a quality, or a relationship by which one measures one's stature or self-worth.

Q

Qualification

A quality, an ability, or an accomplishment that makes a person suitable for a particular position or task.

R

Rejection

To refuse to accept, submit to, believe, or make use of.

Relationship

Connection by blood or marriage; kinship.

Relative

Belonging to the same family; related or compared to each other.

Require

To call for as obligatory or appropriate; demand.

Glossary *(cont.)*

Research
Scholarly or scientific investigation or inquiry.

Respect
A feeling of appreciative, often deferential regard; esteem.

Responsibility
Something for which one is responsible; a duty, an obligation, or a burden.

Résumé
A brief account of one's professional or work experience and qualifications, often submitted with an employment application.

Role Model
A person who serves as a model in a particular behavioral or social role for another person to emulate.

S

Salary
Fixed compensation for services, paid to a person on a regular basis.

Schedule
1. A list of times of departures and arrivals; a timetable.
2. A plan for performing work or achieving an objective, specifying the order and allotted time for each part.

School
1. An institution for the instruction of children or people under college age.
2. An institution for instruction in a skill or business.

Self-Confidence
Confidence in oneself or one's own abilities.

Self-Conscious
Socially ill at ease.

Service
Work done for others as an occupation or a business.

Shopping Mall
A shopping center with stores and businesses facing a system of enclosed walkways for pedestrians.

Sibling
One of two or more individuals having one or both parents in common; a brother or sister.

Similarity
The quality or condition of being similar; resemblance.

Situation
Position or status with regard to conditions and circumstances.

Skill
An art, a trade, or a technique; a developed talent or ability.

Smoking
Engaging in the smoking of tobacco.

Glossary (cont.)

Social
Inclined to seek out or enjoy the company of others; sociable.

Solution
The method or process of solving a problem.

Stable
Consistently dependable.

Staff
A group of assistants to a manager, an executive, or another person in authority.

Stress
A mentally or emotionally disruptive or upsetting condition occurring in response to adverse external influences and capable of affecting physical health, usually characterized by increased heart rate, a rise in blood pressure, muscular tension, irritability, and depression.

Structure
The way in which parts are arranged or put together to form a whole; make-up.

Student
One who attends a school, college, or university.

Study
1. The act or process of studying.
2. The pursuit of knowledge, as by reading, observation, or research.

Substance Abuse
Excessive use of addictive substances, especially alcohol and narcotic drugs. Also called *chemical abuse.*

T

Team
A group organized to work together.

Teenager
A person between the ages of 13 and 19; an adolescent.

Theory
Abstract reasoning.

Thoughtful
Having or showing heed for the well-being or happiness of others and a propensity for anticipating their needs or wishes.

Tobacco
Any of various plants of the genus Nicotiana, especially N. tabacum, native to tropical America and widely cultivated for its leaves, which are used primarily for smoking.

Trust
Firm reliance on the integrity, ability, or character of a person or thing.

Truth
Conformity to fact or actuality.

Try
To make an effort to do or accomplish (something); attempt.

Glossary *(cont.)*

U

Upbringing
The rearing and training received during childhood.

Update
To bring up to date.

Urban
1. Of, relating to, or located in a city.
2. Characteristic of the city or city life.

V

Value
An amount, as of goods, services, or money, considered to be fair and suitable.

Verify
To prove the truth of by presentation of evidence or testimony; substantiate.

Violence
Physical force exerted for the purpose of violating, damaging, or abusing.

Vocation
A regular occupation, especially one for which a person is particularly suited or qualified.

Vulgar
Deficient in taste, delicacy, or refinement.

W

Want Ad
A classified advertisement.

Weakness
A personal defect or failing.

Well-Groomed
1. Attentive to details of dress; meticulously neat.
2. Carefully tended or curried.
3. Trim and tidy.

Work
A job, employment; a trade, profession, or other means of livelihood.

Worthwhile
Sufficiently valuable or important to be worth one's time, effort, or interest.

Bibliography

Adler, Ronald, et. al. *Interplay: The Process of Interpersonal Communications.* Holt, Rinehart and Winston, 1992.

Arthur, W. *An Etymological Dictionary of Family and Christian Names.* Gala Research Co., 1969.

Baker, Michael O. *What Would You Do?* Midwest Publications, 1989.

Baring-Gould, Sabine. *Family Names and Their Stories.* Baltimore Genealogy Publishing Company, 1968.

Beable, W. H. *Epitaphs.* Thomas Y. Crowell Company, 1971.

Bielen, Peggy and Sandy McDaniel. *Project Self-Esteem.* Jalmar Press, 1990.

Borba, Michele. *Esteem Builders.* Jalmar Press, 1989.

Bowman, W. D. *The Story of Surnames.* Gale Research Co, 1968.

Brown, Raymond. *A Book of Epitaphs.* Taplinger Publishing Company, 1969.

California Department of Education. *Caught in the Middle: Educational Reform for Young Adolescents in California Middle Schools.* California State Department of Education, 1987.

Canfield, Jack. *Self-Esteem in the Classroom.* Jack Canfield and Self-Esteem Seminars, 1968.

Canter, Lee. *Homework Without Tears.* Lee Canter and Associates.

Cantril, Hadley. *A Fresh Look at the Human Design: Challenges of Humanistic Psychology.* McGraw Hill, 1967.

Charnock, R. S. *Ludus Patronymicus: Or the Etymology of Surnames.* Gale Research, 1968.

Collins, Randall and Scott Coltrane. *Sociology of Marriage and the Family.* Nelson-Hall Publishers, Inc., 1991.

Davis, Kent. *Million Dollar Machine.* Go-Well Kent, 1990.

Dunn, Rita and Kenneth. *Teaching Students Through Their Individual Learning Style.* Prentice-Hall, 1978.

Dunkling, L. A. *First Names First.* Universe Books, 1977.

Farber, Adrla, and Elaine Mazlish. *How to Talk So Kids Will Listen.* Wade Publishers, 1982.

Fluegeman, Andrew. *The New Book of Games.* Inner Choice Publishing, 1976.

Fluegeman, Andrew. *More New Games.* Inner Choice Publishing, 1981.

Frinder, Gloria. *Learning to Learn.* Incentive Publications, 1990.

Funk-Wagnalls. *Atlas of the Body.* Rand-McNally and Co, 1980.

Gigliotti, Michele. "Working It Out in Writing." *Middle Years Magazine.* Scholastic, Sept./Oct. 1994.

Glenn, H. S. and Nelsen, J. *Raising Self-Reliant Children in a Self-Indulgent World.* Prima Publishing and Communications, 1988.

Bibliography (cont.)

Goldstein, Arnold, et. al. *Skill-Streaming the Adolescent.* Research Press, 1988.

Hanks, Patrick. *A Dictionary of Surnames.* Oxford Press, 1988.

Hauglund, Elaine and Marcia Harris. *On This Day.* Libraries Unlimited, 1983.

Kaiser, Arlene. *Your Students' Self-Esteem.* Presentation, Kreidler, William J. "Practicing Peacemaking". *Instructor Magazine.* April, 1995.

LeMeres, Clare. *The Winner's Circle: Yes I Can.* LeMers Lifestyles Unlimited, 1990.

Mann, Thomas C. and Janet Greene. *Over Their Dead Bodies.* The Stephen Greene Press, 1962.

Molyneux, Lynn. *Cooperative Learning.* Trellis Books, 1986.

Myrick, Robert D. and Joe Wittner. *The Teacher as Facilitator.* Educational Media, 1989.

Niguel Hills Middle School Staff. *Niguel Hills Middle School Student Advisement Curriculum: Grades 6–8,* 1993.

New Book of Knowledge, Vols. C, L, S, ,. Grolier Inc., 1970.

Purkey, W. and J. Novak. *Inviting School Success: A Self-Concept Approach to Teaching and Learning.* Wadsworth Publishing, 1984.

Responsibility Skills: Lessons for Success. Hughes Aircraft, 1990.

Rohnke, Kendall. *Silver Bullets.* Kendall-Hall Publishing Co, 1984.

Rohnke, Kendall. *Cowstails and Cobras II.* Project Adventure, 1989.

Shaw, William. *Social and Personal Ethics.* Wadsworth Publishing, 1993.

Wallis, Charles. *Stories on Stone.* Oxford Press, 1954.

Wolfman, Ira. *Do People Grow on Family Trees? Genealogy for Kids and Other Beginnings.* Workman Publishing, 1991.

Appendix

Teacher Savers

Included in this section are 25 forms designed to help teachers and students. They range in topic from student homework planners to thank-you letters to parent conference logs to classroom discipline mediators designed to focus a student's thoughts carefully on those well-known classroom behaviors—tardiness, rudeness, inappropriate talking, silliness, and failure to follow directions. Many a student has profited by copying the appropriate one when directed to do so by the teacher. A close look at these and other pages will remind the busy teacher of the many times such ready-made guides can become real "teacher savers."

Awards

Included in this section are 12 awards designed to let the teacher acknowledge—swiftly and formally—the many positive actions, attitudes, and accomplishments of his/her students. Having these ready to issue is a real boon to the teacher who wants to bestow a pat on the back at the time it is deserved. It often makes a difference in student attitude (and parental appreciation!) when a hard-working but perhaps otherwise undistinguished student receives recognition. In fact, a major trait of good teachers is their continual desire to motivate students. One proven way to do this is by giving frequent praise and recognition.

Activity Evaluation

Name _____   **Date** _____

1. What activity did you participate in? _____

   _____

2. What was the activity centered around? _____

   _____

3. What was the purpose of the lesson? _____

   _____

4. What was the best or most enjoyable part of the lesson? _____

   _____

5. What suggestions do you have to improve the lesson?_____

   _____

6. What did you contribute to the day's activity? _____

   _____

Self-Evaluation

Grade

_____   a. I was cooperative during the period.

_____   b. I worked quietly.

_____   c. I did my best work.

_____   d. I used the time to the fullest.

_____   e. I contributed to the group effort.

_____   f. I have accurately filled out this sheet.

_____   g. My total grade for the day should be_____ .

Comments:

Classroom Citation

Name _____ Date _____

The following classroom rule has been broken:

☐ 1. talking/disturbing others

☐ 2. fighting/arguing

☐ 3. throwing things

☐ 4. chewing gum or eating in class

☐ 5. running or jumping inside building

☐ 6. misuse of school property

☐ 7. copying other people's work

☐ 8. touching other people's belongings

☐ 9. in classroom without permission

☐ 10. late when the bell rings

Please discuss these offenses with your child.

Teacher _____

Parent Signature _____

Matching Game

(This is a getting-to-know you activity for the beginning of school, letting students find others with shared interests.)

What is your favorite . . .

animal?

book?

song?

color?

food?

place to visit?

movie?

type of shoe?

instrument?

Directions: Write your answers to the questions in the boxes. When your teacher tells you to, check around the room to see how many students wrote the same responses. If you find a match with another student, have that person sign his/her name in the box. See how many matches you can find within your room.

Personal ID Sheets

Name: _____

Address: _____

Home phone: _____

Parents' names: _____

Parents' work phones: _____

Schedule

Period	Teacher	Room #	Subject

Student Helpers!

Attendance _____

_____

Scribes/Recorders _____

_____

Passers/Collectors _____

_____

Organizers _____

_____

Messengers _____

_____

Cleaners _____

_____

Officers of the Class _____

_____

Other _____

_____

_____

_____

Tardiness

What Did I Do?

I was late to class.

How Does My Action Affect the Class?

When I am late to class, I interrupt normal activities. The teacher has to stop teaching to deal with my tardiness. In addition, the students who are trying to learn have to be delayed from learning because of my actions.

How Do My Actions Affect Me?

When I am tardy to class, I miss valuable learning time that is intended to help me succeed in life. When I am tardy, I miss warm-ups which are important to my success in class. In addition, I am setting a bad precedent for my life. In the real world, I would probably get fired if I was tardy to my job without a sufficient reason. Tardiness is also a sign of disrespect to the teacher. Above all, tardiness is a negative influence in my life. Tardiness can also make me fail the course.

What Should I Have Done?

I should have taken care of my concerns in the hallway and made it to class on time. If there is a pressing problem, like going to the bathroom, I should ask the teacher ahead of time so I am not tardy to class.

What Will I Do Next Time?

I will make an effort not to be late to class anymore.

Not Following Directions

What Did I Do?

I did not follow directions.

How Does My Action Affect the Class?

When I do not follow directions, I interrupt normal class activities. The teacher has to stop teaching and deal with my situation. In addition, the students who are trying to learn have to be delayed from learning because of my actions.

How Do My Actions Affect Me?

When I do not follow directions, I choose to interrupt the flow of learning. This hurts my grade, and it hurts my potential for future success. In the real world, my boss will expect me to follow company rules too.

What Should I Have Done?

I should have read or listened to the directions carefully and proceeded to follow them like everybody else.

What Will I Do Next Time?

Next time, if I have a question or concern about the directions, I will raise my hand and ask the teacher. The teacher might understand my confusion and explain the directions differently so I can understand.

Talking

What Did I Do?

I was talking without permission.

How Does My Action Affect the Class?

When I am talking excessively, I interrupt normal class activities. The teacher has to stop teaching and deal with my problem. In addition, the students who are trying to learn have to be delayed from learning because of my actions.

How Do My Actions Affect Me?

By my excessive talk, I show how immaturely I can act. The teacher loses respect for me and has to treat me like a small child. I know I am not a small child, but I will get treated like one when I continue to talk out of turn. The teacher might have to call my parents, and I could be punished.

What Should I Have Done?

I should have raised my hand. The teacher would have called on me, and I could have spoken then. If I needed to communicate to someone else in the classroom, I could have waited until after class.

What Will I Do Next Time?

Next time I will raise my hand to be heard in front of class or wait to speak to my friends after class.

Rudeness

What Did I Do?

I was being rude to another person.

How Does My Action Affect the Class?

Rudeness hurts others' feelings as well as distracts the class from learning. When I am overly rude, I interrupt normal class activities. The teacher has to stop teaching and deal with my rudeness. In addition, the students who are trying to learn have to be delayed from learning because of my actions. The person I was rude to may have hurt feelings.

How Do My Actions Affect Me?

Being rude is a bad reflection on me as a human being. The more badness that I give, the more badness I will get. In addition, rudeness can lower my grade and get me in trouble with my parents.

What Should I Have Done?

If I feel that I should be rude to someone, I should tell the teacher and explain the situation. The teacher will be fair, and I can resolve my conflict peacefully.

What Will I Do Next Time?

I will not be rude to anyone. I know the more love I give, the more love I get.

Silliness

What Did I Do?

I was being annoying by acting silly.

How Does My Action Affect the Class?

When I clown around during a serious part of class, it distracts other members of the class. They have to stop learning and listen to the teacher deal with me. Other students are negatively affected by my actions. They want to learn, but it makes it hard to learn when I am clowning around.

How Do My Actions Affect Me?

By my silliness, I show how immaturely I can act. The teacher loses respect for me and has to treat me like a small child. I know I am not a small child, but I will get treated like one when I continue to be silly. The teacher might have to call my parents, and I could be punished.

What Should I Have Done?

I should keep my silly thoughts and actions to myself or tell a friend during lunch or after school.

What Will I Do Next Time?

I will refrain from annoying the class with my silliness. If I have trouble controlling my silliness, I will tell the teacher so we can resolve the problem.

Conflict Resolution

Persons Involved: _____

Nature of Conflict: _____

Side 1:_____

Side 2:_____

Possible Compromises:

1)

2)

3)

Agreement: Date:_____

_____   _____   _____
Student   Student   Mediator

Cognitive Map Form

This type of diagram is really just a web with spaces for supporting details. It can help us take notes and remember the main points of a lesson.

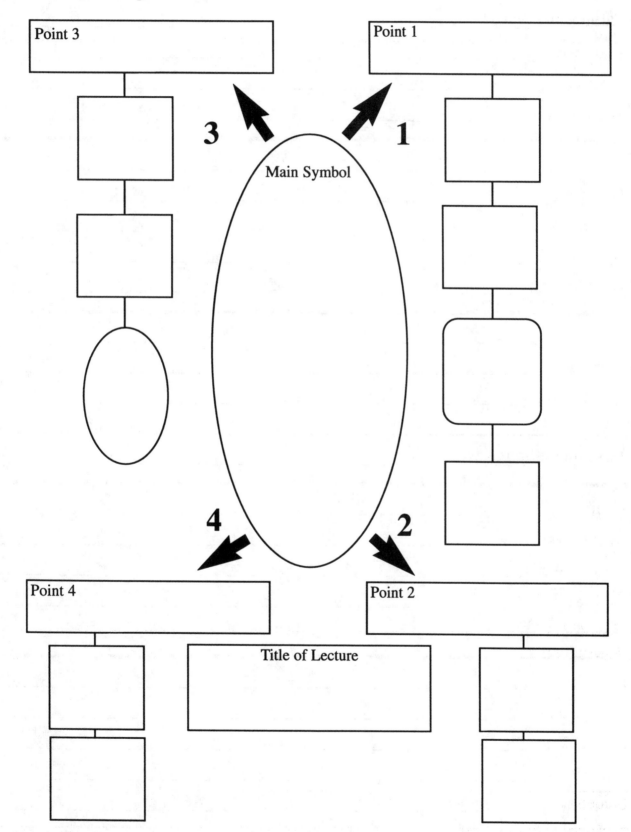

Guest Speakers Matrix

Name: _____

Occupation:_____

Phone: Work_____ Home _____

Address: _____

Used for unit:_____ Date: _____

Name: _____

Occupation:_____

Phone: Work_____ Home _____

Address: _____

Used for unit:_____ Date: _____

Name: _____

Occupation:_____

Phone: Work_____ Home _____

Address: _____

Used for unit:_____ Date: _____

Name: _____

Occupation:_____

Phone: Work_____ Home _____

Address: _____

Used for unit:_____ Date: _____

Name: _____

Occupation:_____

Phone: Work_____ Home _____

Address: _____

Used for unit:_____ Date: _____

Teacher-Parent Warning

Teacher-Parent Warning

Your son or daughter has a deficiency in the following area(s):

- ❑ Needs Extra Practice
- ❑ Has Not Turned in Homework
- ❑ Is Currently Failing
- ❑ Is Not Working to Potential

_____
_____
_____
_____

- ❑ Response Needed

Teacher-Parent Warning

Your son or daughter has a deficiency in the following area(s):

- ❑ Needs Extra Practice
- ❑ Has Not Turned in Homework
- ❑ Is Currently Failing
- ❑ Is Not Working to Potential

_____
_____
_____
_____

- ❑ Response Needed

Teacher-Parent Warning

Your son or daughter has a deficiency in the following area(s):

- ❑ Needs Extra Practice
- ❑ Has Not Turned in Homework
- ❑ Is Currently Failing
- ❑ Is Not Working to Potential

_____
_____
_____

- ❑ Response Needed

Teacher-Parent Warning

Your son or daughter has a deficiency in the following area(s):

- ❑ Needs Extra Practice
- ❑ Has Not Turned in Homework
- ❑ Is Currently Failing
- ❑ Is Not Working to Potential

_____
_____
_____

- ❑ Response Needed

Homework Weekly Planner

Name:_____

Monday		Tuesday	

Wednesday		Thursday	

Weekend Homework

Projects:

Self-Evaluation

Answer the following questions thoughtfully on your own paper.

1. What are my strengths in this class?

2. What are the areas that I need to improve?

3. What are the best things about this class?

4. What are the worst things about this class?

5. Did I try as hard as I could have in this class so far? If not, why?

6. Do I think I've learned a lot in the class?

7. What is the most valuable thing I learned? Why?

8. Have I behaved myself in this class? How?

9. Have I treated others with respect? How?

10. What can I do to continuously improve myself?

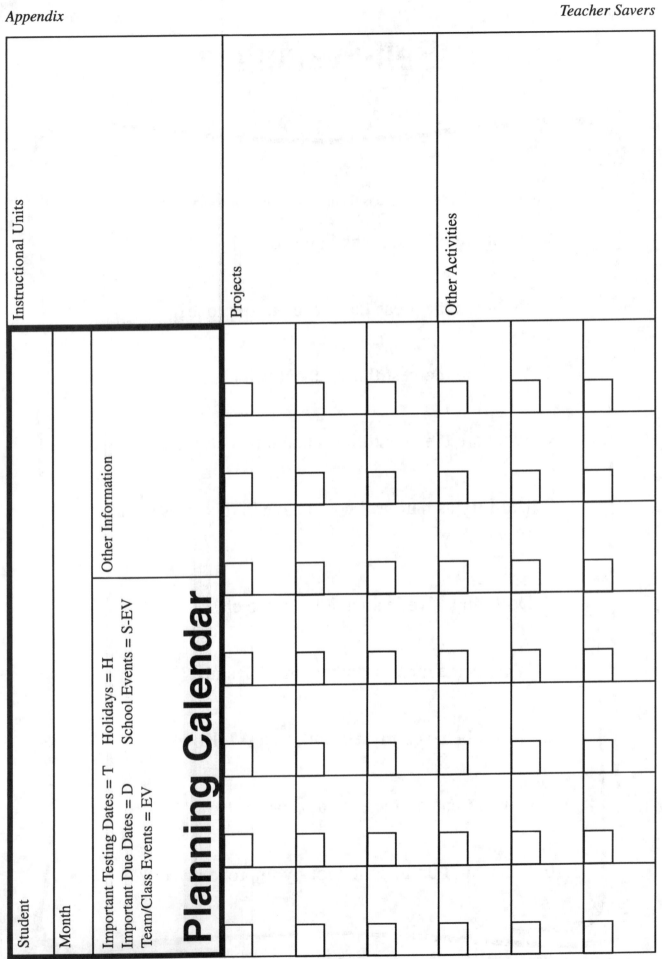

Planning Calendar

Instructional Units

Projects

Other Activities

Student

Month

Important Testing Dates = T   Holidays = H
Important Due Dates = D   School Events = S-EV
Team/Class Events = EV

Other Information

Teacher-Student Conference

Teacher	Date
Student	Others Present
Nature of Concern	

Student Feedback

_____
_____
_____
_____
_____
_____
_____

_____
_____
_____
_____

Resolutions Made

Contract Needed   Yes   No

Parents' Names/Phone Numbers

Parent Conference Needed

Yes   No

College Plans

Liberal Arts
-English
-history
-political science
-government
-economics
-philosophy
-anthropology
-archaeology
-linguistics
-foreign languages
-geography
-humanities
-Latin American studies
-sociology
-religious studies
-classics (Greek-
   Latin, mythology)

Science
-biology
-chemistry
-geology
-astronomy
-botany
-oceanography
-mathematics
-physics
-zoology

Business
-accounting
-finance
-management
-marketing

Communications
-speech
-radio/TV-film
-advertising
-journalism

Fine Arts
-art
-music
-theater
-dance

Professional Schools
-Nursing
-Pharmacy
-Social Work
-Computer Sciences
-Architecture
-Education
-Engineering
-Kinesiology (sports)

Post Graduate
Law
Medicine
Masters
Doctorate

The **major** I would like to pursue is_____

The **minor** I would choose to study would be _____

The college or university I would like to attend would be

_____

Their mascot is the _____

Their school colors are _____

I will finance my college education by (circle one):

Scholarship   School Loan

Grant   My Own Work

Progress Report

Student _____ Date _____

Teacher _____ Subject _____

Commendations	✓	Comment Box
Good Attendance	☐	
Prompt	☐	
Courteous	☐	
Effective Study Habits	☐	
Excellent Achievement	☐	
Attentive in Class	☐	
Participates Well in Class	☐	
Dependable	☐	
Cooperative	☐	
Shows Good Leadership	☐	
Helpful	☐	

Unsatisfactory Comments	✓	Comment Box
Is Currently Failing	☐	
Borderline	☐	
Ineffective Study Habits	☐	
Lack of Work Ethic	☐	
Uncooperative	☐	
Missing Assignments	☐	
Negative Attitude	☐	
Parent Conference Requested	☐	
Lack of Organizational Skills	☐	
Other:	☐	

Library Rules

The library is a special privilege. You can find magazines, newspapers, books, audio tapes, videos, and even computer services! If you don't observe these simple rules, the library privilege will no longer be an option for you.

1 **Use Quiet Voices**

Disturbing others is rude.

2 **Know How to Find What You Are Looking For**

- periodicals index
- card catalog
- reference
- telecommunications
- casual reading

3 **Exercise Your Individuality— Do Individual Work**

- notes
- worksheets
- bibliographies

4 **Know How to Check Out Library Materials**

Ask your librarian politely to check out a book and fill out the book card appropriately.

5 **Avoid Late Fines—Turn In Books on Time**

If you don't return your books, you will be unable to use the library and may have to pay money for being late.

Don't forget these 5 rules, and the wonders of the library will be in your grasp!

Parent Phone Record

Student	Parent Who Was Contacted	Date	Answering Machine?

Summary of Conversation

Student	Parent Who Was Contacted	Date	Answering Machine?

Summary of Conversation

Parent Conference Log

Student _____

Date _____

Parent(s) Present _____

Other Members Present _____

Student's Positive Aspects

Concerns

Possible Solutions

Contract Needed?
Yes   No

Parent Conference Sign Up

Teacher_____

Please list your name and phone number and indicate whether you would like to discuss the progress of your child over the telephone or in person.

Parents' names	Student's name	Phone numbers (W/H)	Conference by phone or in person?

Thank You, Parents!

Date:_____

To:_____

From:_____

I just wanted to take some time and say "thanks" for your help recently!

It is parents like you who make our schools a great place to learn!

I can speak for everybody when I say you really made a quality difference. Don't just take it from me—here are the students:

The Hard Worker Award

presented to

in appreciation for

Date

Signed

The Sunshine Award

presented to

_____

in appreciation for

_____

Date _____

Signed _____

Certificate of Award

_____

is awarded this certificate of
*Notable Accomplishment in
Recognition of Helpfulness*

_____

_____

Signed _____

This _____ day of_____

Certificate of Award

is awarded this certificate of

_____

Notable Accomplishment
in Recognition of Accuracy

This _____ day of _____

Signed _____

The Mechanical Genius Award

presented to

_____

in appreciation for

_____

Signed _____

Date _____

Leadership!

This award is presented to

for

Date

Signed

Certificate of Accomplishment

_____

is awarded this certificate

for

Reaching a Goal

This _____ day of _____

Signed _____

The Original Thinker

This Award Is Presented to

_____

for Unique Originality

Signed _____

Date _____

Comments:

The Writing Award

Offered to

_____

for Notable Accomplishment

Signed _____

Date _____

The Good Sportsmanship Award

presented to

Date

Signed

Perfect Attendance

This Certificate Is Awarded

to

to _____.

for the Period of _____

Signed _____

Date _____

The Teacher's Special Award

is presented to

_____

in recognition of

_____

Signed _____

Date _____